FROM ROOT TO RAIN

Dr Sneha Verghese is a double postgraduate in Biotechnology and Journalism, and holds a PhD in Mass Communication and Journalism. She works for the Indian Council of Agricultural Research, but her passion is writing. While science writing is her forte, she has been a freelance writer and columnist for various newspapers and magazines, and her literary work has appeared in well-acclaimed anthologies. Sneha lives in Hyderabad.

FROM ROOT TO RAIN

Hidden Stories of Nature's Science

SNEHA VERGHESE

Illustrations by Ishan Trivedi

hachette INDIA

First published in paperback in 2025 by Hachette India
(Registered name: Hachette Book Publishing India Pvt. Ltd)
An Hachette UK company
www.hachetteindia.com

1

Versions of the essays in this book first appeared in the *Young Hans* supplement of *The Hans India* in the column 'Nature Narratives' between 2015 and 2018, and are included with the permission of the newspaper.

Illustrations by Ishan Trivedi

Photographs of Fritz Haber and Carl Bosch on Page 28 have been sourced from Wikimedia Commons Public Domain.

ISBN 978-93-5731-416-9

Hachette Book Publishing India Pvt. Ltd
4th & 5th Floors, Corporate Centre
Plot No. 94, Sector 44, Gurugram – 122003, India

Typeset by Manmohan Kumar, Delhi

Printed and bound in India
by Thomson Press India Ltd.

FSC www.fsc.org MIX Paper | Supporting responsible forestry FSC® C010615

To
my aunt
Asha

For making me a lover of stories
and
a writer of them too.

CONTENTS

1

THE 'ROOT' OF A DISASTER

'I'm not helping out in the fields today,' said Maria, standing at the door of their small hovel, with an air of importance. 'I am wearing my new dress, and I must not spoil it. I must look my best when we go to the fair this evening!'

'Well, it's not evening yet, sister,' said her older brother Nolan, giving her a gentle push. 'You'll still have to help.'

'Why? Oh...why?' groaned Maria. 'Can't I just have a holiday? I already finished my work at the cloth mill for today. Do I have to work in the fields too?'

'There are no holidays when you're poor, Maria,' came Maria's mother's voice. 'And more so when we work on somebody else's land. You know how angry the landlord will be with your father if we don't finish our share of work for today.'

'Be careful with that dress, child,' scolded her father. 'That's got to last you for another three or four years.' He walked out of their hovel, while Maria stood by and sulked.

'It's only a dress from a local shop selling hand-me-downs,' she muttered. 'And far too big for me anyway.'

'We used half our savings on it, lass,' said her mother gravely. 'And what do you do? You refuse to work!'

'I never said I wouldn't work,' said Maria, going red in the face. 'I suppose I should change out of this and wear one of my old dresses and that tattered pinafore again,' she sighed.

Her mother glared at her, but did not say anything.

I wish we weren't so poor, thought Maria as she put on her old frock again and adjusted her frayed bonnet. *I suppose things couldn't get any worse.*

It was the year 1845 and, unknown to them, things were about to get much worse.

Fourteen-year-old Maria and her family were poor farm labourers in the county of Cork in southern Ireland, where they worked on the potato fields of the rich landlords. They hardly had enough to eat. The children were unschooled too as their parents couldn't afford to send them to study. While eighteen-year-old Nolan worked as a chimney sweep, Maria helped out at a local textile mill.

When Maria joined Nolan on the way to the potato fields, he told her, 'I heard that Eric is going to the

village school now. I suppose a bit of education might make him rise above the problems of our lot.'

'Oh, I don't think so,' said Maria cheerfully. 'He doesn't seem to care all that much. I know I couldn't be much bothered with studying; I would probably be the bottom of the class. I wonder what they study there.'

'Oh, I know,' said Nolan. 'Reading, 'riting and 'rithmetic.'

'What's 'rithmetic?' asked Maria.

'If I knew that, I wouldn't be working here on these fields, would I?' retorted Nolan.

The two set about helping with the potato harvest. Summer was almost upon them, and this would be the last crop before the season changed. Their meals consisted of potatoes and nothing else; that was the cheapest food they could afford. They had heard their parents recalling the 'good old days' when oats and milk had been affordable, but now it was beyond the reach of the Irish poor.

'Something seems to be wrong with these plants,' remarked Maria to Nolan as she set about her work. 'Look at these brown spots on the leaves! And they seem to be spreading too.'

'All the plants have them,' said Nolan. 'The potatoes seem alright.'

Maria glanced doubtfully at the potatoes. 'They have some dark patches,' she said.

'Some of these leaves have shrivelled, though,' said Nolan, carefully examining the plants. 'These...seem to be rotting away. The stems too.'

'Maybe we should tell Father,' Maria said. 'And he can inform the landlord. What if it's a disease?'

But their father brushed it aside, saying, 'The landlord would laugh at me or tell me to keep my nose out of such matters.'

However, at the children's insistence, the poor man approached the landlord. But as predicted, his employer was rude and ordered him to get back to work on the fields.

***

Work went on as usual, and a few weeks passed before they heard the news. All the harvested potatoes that had been stored had gone rotten!

'I told you there was something suspicious about those potatoes,' whispered Maria to Nolan, as they stood among the crowd outside the storerooms, holding their noses. The foul stench was unbearable.

'The rot started from the skins and spread inside the tubers,' said their father that evening. 'I spoke to the labourers from the other fields too. It's the same everywhere. Most of the potatoes harvested this time are rotten. Gone.'

'Ah, well, the crop just failed *this* time,' consoled their mother. 'Next season we might get a better harvest.'

Summer was a lean season for potatoes anyway, so the family didn't suffer much. They still had some potatoes stored away, left over from the previous season, and some salted pork.

But the next potato crop failed too! It was the same – a fungal growth that rotted the plant from the inside and infected the tubers – called the 'potato blight' disease. Things became difficult for Maria and her family. Nolan tried to find more work, but nobody was ready to give him any because everybody seemed to be struggling for money. The family tried selling some of their possessions, but they were far too few and far too invaluable to get them anything more than a little money to buy oats for a few days. It was the same at every poor Irish person's home; starvation was setting in.

***

Three years passed. The family couldn't find work anymore. The potato crops had failed season after season, and the land was affected by a great famine. The landlord refused to pay them or provide them with food. Maria and Nolan's parents saved up every morsel for them, going hungry themselves. Their starvation led to sickness and, soon, their father died, followed by their mother. The landlord showed no mercy. He evicted Nolan and Maria from the little shack, and they were left to fend for themselves out on the streets.

'People are leaving Ireland,' said Nolan sadly to Maria. 'Maybe we too should go and try our luck elsewhere. What do you think?'

Maria nodded, sobbing.

'I have arranged with a kind family to take you with them to Dublin,' said Nolan. 'Try to find work as a housekeeper in one of the homes of the royal families. At least you will not go hungry.'

'But what about you?' asked Maria. 'Won't you come with us?'

Nolan looked away. 'They don't have enough food to feed two mouths, and I have no money to give them,' he said. 'Don't worry about me, Maria. I have found another way out.'

That night, both slept on the streets, under a tree. Maria couldn't sleep well. She dreamt of her childhood, her parents, and cried in her sleep when she thought about separating from Nolan.

A loud commotion woke her up. It was already morning, and a crowd had gathered. The police were taking away a young man by the scruff of his neck.

Maria realized it was Nolan! She ran behind them. 'Nolan! What happened? Why are they taking you away?'

'He broke into his landlord's house,' one of the policemen shouted out at her.

'Getting caught was my plan, Maria,' Nolan whispered. 'I'll be sent to a prison in Australia, where I will not starve.' Maria watched helplessly as she watched Nolan being taken away, never to see him again.

How could the lack of potatoes cause a famine in an entire country?

The potato (*Solanum tuberosum*) is native to Peru in South America and was introduced in Ireland by Spanish conquistadors in 1590. However, it soon became a popular crop as it was cheap, and nutritious as well. Potatoes are rich in carbs and are a good source for energy needed for hard physical work. It is also rich in potassium and vitamin C. When the famine struck in 1845, more than 8 million people depended on potatoes as their staple meal, and people in the rural areas could afford almost nothing except potatoes.

'The Great Famine', or 'The Great Hunger', which occurred between 1845 and 1849, was a great disaster in Ireland's history, with the culprit being a fungus called *Phytophthora infestans*, which causes the 'Late Blight' disease in potato plants.

Ships from North America to England carried the fungus to Dublin and soon the fungus spread to large areas that had potato cultivation. The fungus caused potato leaves to turn black with a watery rot, starting with brown freckles of patches on the leaves, which slowly spread. When potatoes were pulled out of the ground, they appeared fine but rotted very soon. The insides of the tubers would turn brown, starting from the skin, and would finally turn into a soggy, foul-smelling mass.

In just four years, over a million of Ireland's population died from disease and starvation, and through forced migration, Ireland's population came down by another two million.

Potato blight is still a difficult disease to control, because potatoes do not have 'seeds' and the potato tubers must themselves be used to grow the next crop. If the tubers are infected with the fungus but go undetected, the next crop too fails.

2

THE UNSEEN ENEMY

It was morning again, and the sun was shining through the trees in a forest in Thailand. The ants living in the hollow of a tree, which was located at the edge of the jungle, were already foraging for food, stopping at intervals to talk about where more could be found. But Aroon the ant was feeling very strange that day. He felt unwell. He didn't want to go out at all. But what would the other ants say?

'Being sick' was a joke. His leader often said, 'Only humans fall sick. Lazy creatures!' Ants either lived or died. If you lived, you worked non-stop, and if you died, it was because you were stomped to death or eaten up by a larger animal.

As Aroon hurried out unwillingly to finish his daily chores, he wondered what could have made him sick. He had eaten some strange-looking reddish-grey spores the previous day. Was that it?

As he went on, he found himself becoming more and more dizzy. He couldn't walk straight. His friends Lilly and Chaisee were coming from the opposite direction.

'Hi, Aroon,' they said, waving.

All of a sudden, Aroon felt a strange force come over him, and he rushed forward to greet them, with a huge smile, 'Hellooooo, friendsss...' He bumped into them, knocked them down and went on in his crazy way.

Lilly and Chaisee were puzzled. Aroon was a very quiet and shy ant otherwise, and here he was being overfriendly.

'What's wrong with him?' wondered Chaisee.

'Looks like he's lost his marbles!' said Lilly.

Aroon, meanwhile, had strayed away from his regular trail and was heading into the forest. He was feeling fuzzy, and baffled about his own behaviour. Why had he spoken like that? He knew he was going the wrong way. But he couldn't stop himself. Some unknown force inside his head guided him deeper and deeper into the forest.

He couldn't think anymore. Surrounded by huge trees, plants and moss, he felt happy, and at peace...all he wanted now was to find a leaf.

He looked around and saw a big, plump, green leaf growing on a low branch of a tree. He headed happily towards it, as if remote-controlled, his mind no longer his own. He climbed on to its underside, settled himself at the centre, and dug his mouth into the leaf's vein.

As he sucked the juices from the leaf slowly, his mind blanked out. Nothing mattered anymore.

***

Three weeks passed. Aroon had not returned to the anthill.

Lilly was worried. 'Let's look for him, Chaisee,' she said.

'He must have lost his way in the forest,' Chaisee remarked, and both headed towards the forest.

Deep inside, they searched frantically for him. 'Look, there he is, hanging on to that leaf!' cried Chaisee. But

when they went closer, Lilly let out a gasp of horror. Aroon was very still, and growing out of his head was a long tube-like structure.

'Run!' cried Lilly. But before they could run, the strange tube burst and showered reddish grey spores all over them...

Was the little ant dead?

Yes, sadly, it was.

Ophiocordyceps unilateralis, more commonly known as *Cordyceps* fungi, is a parasitic fungal species that preys on insects and is commonly found in tropical forest ecosystems. Also called the zombie-ant fungus, *Cordyceps* infects ants through its spores, and grows inside the body of the ant, releasing chemicals that allow it to control the ant's brain. This usually happens when the spore attaches to the body of an ant, and grows to break open its exoskeleton to gain control of it. It forces the ant to leave its colony and move to moist, humid places (conditions suitable for fungal growth) and station itself on the underside of a leaf, holding on to it with its mandibles (lower jaws) till it dies. *Cordyceps*, however, can infect only the Camponotini tribe of ants. But before you heave a sigh of relief, beware! There are many varieties of the zombie fungus, each of which infects a different host!

3

THE TIME TRACKER WITHIN

The town of Tempus started bustling with activity early at five in the morning every day. The townspeople all awoke at the same time, for a huge gong sounded every morning. They meticulously finished their household chores and rushed to work at seven o' clock sharp, which actually created more problems. Everyone wanted to reach on time and they would all get stuck in traffic for an hour or two!

In the afternoon, the big gong clanged again at one, for lunch break. Exactly at six in the evening, the gong sounded again and everyone set out for home. At ten in the night, the town of Tempus went to sleep.

The gong always sounded from a bell attached to an enormous hourglass placed right in the centre of the city, called the 'Time Tracker'. A special 'timekeeper' was appointed to turn the hourglass upside down every twelve hours, at midnight and noon. It was also his job to make sure that the gong sounded at the right times, based on the markings on the hourglass that measured the level of sand. This kept the entire town on its toes, helping them stick to their timetable.

'It has always been this way,' the people of Tempus would say to outsiders who cared to visit this strange place. 'Now, if you'll excuse us, we have work to do, and we need to get it done on time!' They never had a moment to waste. If anything, the townsfolk worshipped time.

They also revered a strange hermit who was rumoured to live below the Time Tracker, somewhere underground. No living person in Tempus had seen the hermit, and they had only heard stories about him and his wisdom from their grandparents and great-grandparents. Another legend that the residents of Tempus believed in was that the destruction of the hourglass would bring upon them a great calamity, of darkness and chaos, a world without time; and that would be the end of them all.

***

When Rebellis was born, her parents had named her so because she had arrived in the world much later than the due date given by the hospital.

True to her name, Rebellis grew up to be quite a rebel. Though her parents had taught her the rules of the town as soon as she was old enough to understand them, she simply wouldn't follow them. It wasn't really on purpose; it just happened. While everyone woke at five, she would wake up only by seven. Screaming and scolding, her mother would somehow manage to get her ready for school on time. But Rebellis would dawdle around and get late, and the school bus driver would lose his patience every day.

When she did arrive at school, she wouldn't come down to the assembly in time. If she did, then she wouldn't follow the class back upstairs like the other children; she would take a detour, stop by the kindergarten to make faces at the toddlers, smell the flowers in the school garden and wave at friends in other classrooms, before heading to her own class. Of course, she was late for every single class.

When school got over, Rebellis missed the bus home several times. So she often walked back all alone, but she rather enjoyed it. With no one to push her to reach 'on time', she could enjoy the scenery, watch people around her, listen to them talking and discover new routes to her home. At night, she simply wouldn't fall asleep at ten, while everyone else did. If all of this wasn't enough to vex her family, she would ask a number of questions, which her parents couldn't answer.

'What is time?'

'Why is it so necessary to stick to a particular time for everything?'

'What will happen if the hourglass breaks?'

'Why will a calamity befall us?'

'How does the hermit look?'

Unfortunately, Rebellis hated schoolwork too, and this was what led to the 'Great Catastrophe'.

***

As per the rules, Rebellis could only play for an hour after school, after which she was supposed to study. But that day, she had been playing a particularly good game of cricket, and her team had been winning. So it quite upset her when her friends quietly dropped their bats and balls at the stroke of six, and turned to go home.

'Hey, can't we just finish this game?' she shouted, but no one looked at her. Rebellis was annoyed. She was in no mood to study. She went all the way to the town centre, where the Time Tracker stood.

'I hate you!' she screamed loudly several times, quite unmindful of the stares she was getting. 'I don't want to be on time, do you hear?' She threw her ball with all her strength at it, and it hit the glass.

A loud crack reverberated through the town and brought life to a standstill. The Time Tracker was broken! The timekeeper of the town panicked. Sand started seeping out from the broken hourglass, and the gong attached to the hourglass fell with a loud, eerie clang. Such a thing had never happened before, and now it looked like the 'calamity' was inevitable. People gathered there, wailing and fearful. Rebellis herself was too shocked to react, for she hadn't imagined the hourglass would break.

'We are done for,' cried an old man.

'How will we know when to wake up now?' cried another. 'How will we know when to sleep?'

'We won't be able to finish any of our work on time!' lamented another.

'It was her!' shouted the Timekeeper, pointing at Rebellis. 'She did it!'

Before Rebellis could run away, the townsfolk had caught her and brought her to the base of the broken hourglass.

'Punish her!' someone in the crowd shouted, and everyone took up the cry. 'Banish her from Tempus, or we will all die!'

Tears ran down Rebellis's face. They were going to throw her out of the town! She wouldn't be able to see her parents or her home again!

Just then a loud, strong voice from the depths of the earth called out...

'STOP!'

A man in brown robes, with a white, flowing beard, had emerged out of nowhere.

'The hermit!' exclaimed the timekeeper in awe. 'We bow to you, O great one!' The townsfolk fell to their knees.

The hermit looked far from pleased. 'How foolish can you get?' he asked angrily. 'Did you think that banishing a poor child would make everything alright?'

Then he turned to Rebellis and asked her kindly. 'Why did you break the hourglass, child?'

'I was upset,' said Rebellis. 'I wanted to play for some more time, but then the gong struck, and no one would play anymore. I can't wake up early like the others, or sleep on time. I don't know why. I really can't stick to the rules laid down by an hourglass!'

'Hmm,' said the hermit, squinting at her. 'That's not a bad thing, you know – everyone works at a different pace – it's all fine as long as you get enough rest and sleep, and also spend sufficient time on work and play. The rules needn't be applied so strictly. Things can be flexible.'

The townsfolk were horrified. How could anything be *flexible*?

'But – but...' stammered the timekeeper. 'We need the Time Tracker to tell us when to wake up and when to sleep and—'

'You're all mistaken,' said the hermit. 'You've been too dependent on the Time Tracker. Do you realize there's a clock inside each one of you? Your body has a certain rhythm. It knows how to keep time far better than any Time Tracker made of glass and sand. Just like sand collects and empties out in this hourglass, a particular timekeeping protein called 'PER' collects in your body cells during the night and gets broken down during the day, and this is how it knows the time. Haven't you seen the birds of the sky, the insects at your feet? Do you think they listen to your silly gong? They know when it is time to work, and when it is time to rest. Their bodies know it.'

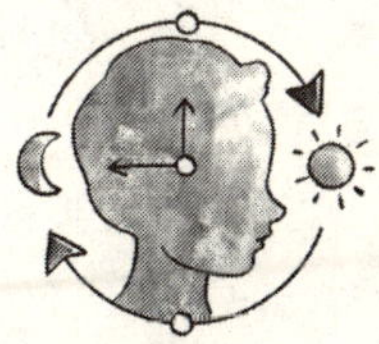

For the first time in centuries, the town of Tempus went to sleep without a gong sounding bedtime. And they found they could all wake up in the morning without much difficulty too, thanks to their own internal body clock!

The Time Tracker was never replaced, and Rebellis was relieved that she no longer had to wake up at five in the morning.

Does our body know the time?

In all living organisms, there is an internal biological clock, called the 'circadian' clock, which helps our bodies to work in rhythm with the environment around us. A circadian rhythm is any biological process that works on a 24-hour cycle, which matches the earth's 24-hour day–night cycle.

While every cell in the body has its own circadian clock, the master clock is a region called the 'suprachiasmatic nucleus' in the hypothalamus (a part of the brain), which monitors the timely functions of the body as a whole.

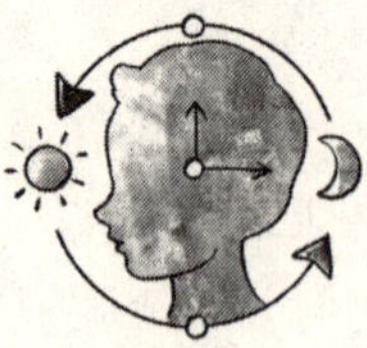

The 2017 Nobel Prize for Medicine was awarded to Jeffrey C. Hall, Michael Rosbash and Michael W. Young, who worked out the molecular and biochemical mechanism of the functioning of this body clock. Using fruit flies as a model organism, they identified a gene that directs the production of a protein 'PER' – which stacks up in the cells during the night, and gets broken down during the day, thus signalling the onset of day and night to the body.

Later, more molecules that helped in this process were identified. Another protein, TIM, binds to the PER protein and takes it inside the cell nucleus. When the PER protein reaches a certain concentration, its production is stopped. Another protein, called DBT, controls how frequently such regulation is carried out, helping cells to adjust to the 24-hour cycle.

Our inner circadian clock helps us adapt to the different phases of the day by regulating our hormones, behaviour, temperature, metabolism and sleep patterns. A significant mismatch between our body clock and external environment can upset our health and well-being.

4

TRAPPED FOR THE LARGER GOOD

Nothing would make Nitrogen change his mind. Poor Mr Haber and Mr Bosch were at their wit's end, but Nitrogen simply refused to cooperate. Both the scientists were trying to make ammonia artificially in the lab from Nitrogen and Hydrogen, but it wasn't working.

Before he arrived at Mr Haber and Mr Bosch's lab, everyone had tried to reason with him, the plants most of all. 'Look, we need you, so that we can grow,' said the eggplant. 'You better decide to behave.' Nitrogen gave her a hard look and turned away with his nose in the air.

'Don't be so harsh with him!' cried the roses, who needed Nitrogen more than the eggplant.

'Won't you do it for us, please, Nitrey?' they cooed together, shaking their beautiful pink, red and yellow petals.

Nitrogen glanced at them, but then turned away again. 'No.'

'But you have to do it for us, pleaaassseee,' cried the corncobs. 'You know it's because you won't give us a hand on your own that we're begging you to join someone else and then help!'

'Hmmph...why should I?' he responded unfeelingly. Nitrogen hated talking. He hated making friends. He hated being paired with other elements to become something new. Even moving around seemed a waste of time and effort to him. It didn't help that he was the most widely found element in the earth's atmosphere; he just didn't want to mix!

He knew the plants needed him in order to grow well, and that they couldn't absorb him directly from the atmosphere. But he was in a very stable form, with two atoms held together by three bonds, and he didn't see any point in breaking up to form bonds with hydrogen and oxygen. Unfortunately for the plants, they could take in Nitrogen only if he joined with Hydrogen to form Ammonia, or joined with oxygen to form Nitrates or Nitrites.

'You're so selfish,' grumbled the tomatoes and the cucumbers grumpily. 'Here we are, begging you to team up with oxygen or hydrogen, and you're acting all pricey.'

'Look, you guys get enough of me when it rains and even otherwise. I know you all give shelter to those creepy-crawly bacteria that make ammonia out of me, by forcing me to join the Hydrogens. And I also know that lightning during the rains turns at least some of us Nitrogen molecules into nitrates and nitrites. So there! Don't put on an act. I'm not going to make any humans happy by doing what they tell me to.'

'But if you listen to them, you'll be so useful to all of us, don't you see?' said wise old lettuce. 'If they could just convert you into a form that would make it easy for us to absorb you, we could all do so much better together! And you know we all hate that guano so much,' she added in an undertone.

'Guano?' Nitrogen was puzzled. 'What's that?'

'Tell him,' said the roses to the lettuce, wrinkling up their noses in disgust.

'Guano is – er – that thing, you know – from South America – of seabirds, and bats, and other birds—'

'What exactly do you mean – "that thing"?' Nitrogen was curious.

'Ah, it's the – the excrement—'

'What?' asked Nitrogen. 'I don't understand,' he said mischievously, though he understood perfectly well.

'Say it in simpler terms,' urged the tomatoes. 'Not with your high-end vocabulary.'

'Oh, fine,' said the lettuce, a bit annoyed. 'It's – it's bird droppings—'

Nitrogen let out a squeal of laughter.

'Oh yes, you can laugh,' said the cucumbers. 'It's we who suffer that horrible smell when our farmers give us "Best Quality Guano Fertilizer"!'

'Our beautiful perfume is eclipsed by that revolting stench,' exclaimed the roses, and Nitrogen doubled up with laughter. 'Serve you right,' he pouted. 'And just to let you know, Ammonia stinks too.'

'Oh, why do you have to be so mean?' the roses cried. 'We could bear with a synthetic stench, but not real excrement! Couldn't you just be nice for once and help us out?'

Nitrogen refused to answer, and put into practice exactly what he had said to the plants when he reached Haber and Bosch's lab in Germany. He gave the poor scientists a hard time.

'Do you think we should give up?' asked Dr Bosch to Dr Haber one day. 'The stress is getting too much for me.'

'Well, let's try one last time,' said Dr Haber. 'We'll give it up if it doesn't work.'

Nitrogen felt all smug. He had foiled all their efforts at making him bond with Hydrogen. That lowly, one-electron element! What a waste! And if he did, he would have to bond with three of them, not even one. Phooey! Who would do that?

***

Meanwhile, someone else was watching Dr Haber's lab closely. A man peeped into the lab while the scientists were out for lunch, quickly taking notes and passing on the information to his friend at the window. 'They're

trying to make Ammonia in the lab,' he said excitedly to his friend .

'Say, wouldn't this be a wonderful present for the army chief?' his friend replied gleefully.

'The preparations for the war are in full swing,' said the first man. 'This just might help us to make enough ammonia, with which we can make explosives.'

'Yeah, it would be much better than having to use that guano, from which we make gunpowder,' said his friend.

Now, Nitrogen noticed the two whispering and strained to hear what they were saying. The first man jumped back outside to join his friends, and Nitrogen was too busy tracking them to notice that Haber and

Bosch were back and had restarted their experiment. Before he knew it, the temperature had gone up to 500°C, and the pressure was 25 megapascals. *Whoosh!* Nitrogen found himself, a single atom, bonded to three grinning Hydrogen atoms. They had become Ammonia!

'How did it work this time?' asked Nitrogen, flabbergasted.

'I did it,' came a voice. It was Iron! 'I was the catalyst that helped you join the Hydrogens and form Ammonia!'

Nitrogen was too angry to speak. He sulked while the scientists celebrated the 'Haber–Bosch' process, as they named it – the artificial method to make ammonia in large amounts.

The following year, the same process was used on an industrial scale to produce ammonia for use in war explosives, as World War I was going on. But, soon after, the process started being used to produce ammonia fertilizers for plants.

'No more guano!' giggled the roses. as disgruntled Nitrogen, packaged as Ammonia, but still quite smelly, was emptied into their flowerpots.

Why is ammonia important to us?

Ammonia (NH_3) is a colourless pungent gas familiar to us as the smell of pee. It is made up of a single nitrogen atom and three hydrogen atoms. It is common in animal waste, particularly among aquatic organisms, and plays an important role in metabolism and synthesis of fertilizers. Ammonia forms the basic building block in the manufacturing process of several pharmaceutical products and is an ingredient in many commercial cleaning products. However, it is not common in Nature and is available in the form of salt deposits.

Nitrogen, which is a part of ammonia, plays a critical role in the biochemistry of every living thing. It is also the most common gas in our atmosphere (making up 78 per cent of it). But plants and animals can't extract it directly from the air. Nitrogen-fixing bacteria in the soil

Fritz Haber

Carl Bosch

can convert nitrogen to ammonia, but this alone may not suffice. Thus, agriculture was severely affected by a lack of enough nitrogen in the soil for plants.

In 1910, German chemists Fritz Haber and Carl Bosch invented the Haber–Bosch process for combining atmospheric nitrogen and hydrogen into ammonia, under high temperature and high pressure, and using iron as a catalyst. However, this technique was first used by Germany during World War I, as ammonia is vital to produce nitric acid, an important ingredient in explosives. Only later was this process used for large-scale production of ammonia fertilizers.

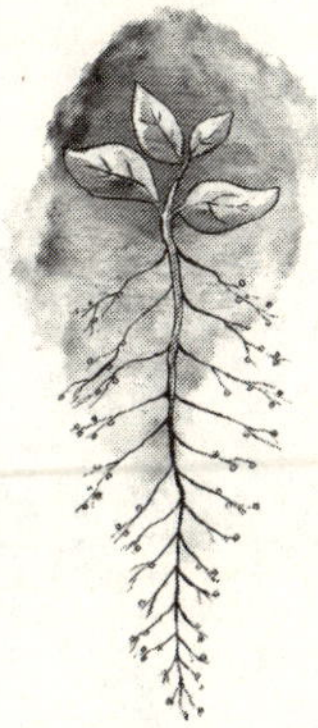

5

WHAT THE ORACLE SAID

'All hail the Oracle!' cried the animals. 'Hail!'

The fox, swathed strangely in green vines, sat atop a rock, his eyes half closed, as if in a deep trance. Most animals of the forest and the surrounding lowlands were assembled at the foot of the rock, paying obeisance to him.

Slowly, the fox lifted a hand to his forehead and let out a moan. 'Aaaah!'

A hush fell on the audience. 'Danger!' shrieked the fox. 'Grave danger!'

'Where, Master, where?' cried the woodpecker, looking around in alarm.

'There!' continued the fox in his high-pitched, hysterical voice. 'There, where the water flows from sky to earth!'

The fox often spoke in cryptic, puzzling sentences like this one, and it was up to the animals to figure out what he really meant.

'Where the water flows from sky to earth...hmm... the waterfall!' cried the weasel.

'Danger...to all of us...rush...now...' muttered the fox, and the big brown bear charged off to the waterfall. The eagle accompanied him, while the rest of the creatures waited with bated breath.

An hour later, the bear was back, triumphant and singing praises of the fox all the way. 'Master is all-seeing, all-knowing,' he shouted. 'Hail to our Master, the Oracle!' completed the eagle.

'What happened?' demanded the other animals. 'Tell us!'

'We found some humans camping out there by the waterfall,' said the excited eagle. 'Brother Bear here was able to scare them away!'

'And in time too!' said the Bear. 'Just imagine, if they had caught any of us? It's all thanks to our Master that we are safe today!'

The animals took up their chant again. 'All hail the Oracle! All hail the Master!'

The fox smiled to himself. He had found the easiest way to lead his life without doing any hard work at all. It had all started with a small prediction he made, though it had just been a stroke of luck. When a family of white-tailed deer had gone missing, the fox had, by chance, seen some poachers shutting them in a cage just outside the forest.

Back in animal territory, he declared that he had had a divine vision from the Almighty – of the family of deer being trapped in cages. The bigger animals immediately rushed to the spot, and to their astonishment, found the deer exactly the way the fox had described.

To his extraordinary good luck, the entire episode turned out in his favour, with the animals believing that he had the divine gift of communicating with God. Since then, he was their 'Oracle,' who could predict calamities and come up with solutions. The fox, on his part, kept up with his act by snooping around everywhere as best as he could, and coming up with one prediction or the other.

Now the fox slowly opened his eyes and raised his hands in blessing. 'I shall always do my best for all of you,' he said in a slow drawl, with an air of importance. 'The Supreme Power communicates with me, and I, with you...' He folded his hands. This was the cue for the audience to make their offerings of fruit, meat and drink to him.

The fox acknowledged all their gifts with a small smile. Suddenly, his face took on a grave look and he said, 'I think someone has once again forgotten to give his offering.'

The other animals looked fearful. 'Who is it, Master?' said the hare, trembling.

'It is that star-nosed joker – the mole – as usual,' said the fox. 'He will bring doom upon you all, if he continues to thwart the Oracle!' muttered the fox darkly.

The animals looked around. The star-nosed mole was nowhere to be seen. They scurried around to find some extra food and offered it to the fox. 'Do not be displeased, Master,' they cried. 'Take this offering! Do not curse us!'

The fox grimly closed his eyes once again. After what seemed an eternity, he spoke up. 'The Oracle is pleased,' he said, with a wave of his hand. 'You may all disperse.'

***

Relieved that they had all been saved from a grave danger, the creatures went back to their regular routine, a few of them complaining about the mole's behaviour. The bear was very annoyed, as he had complete faith in the fox's divine powers. He went to the marshes and called out to the mole.

'Come out this very minute, you silly clown!' he growled. 'We've had enough of you and your star-shaped nose! We won't stand your impertinence anymore!'

The star-nosed mole was a blind creature who usually did not venture out during the day as he lived underground. He had a nose shaped like a star, with tentacle-like projections that gave him a weird look, and this made him the butt of all jokes. This, of course, was one more reason why he didn't mix much with others.

He especially had no respect for the fox who had always been an archenemy of his, waiting for a chance to eat him up. He was sure that the fox was just taking everyone for a ride, and refused to bow down. This infuriated the fox no end, as every other animal was now under his thumb.

The bear kept calling, and finally the mole came out. ‘You have to be present with an offering at the next meeting, do you understand?’ snarled the bear.

‘Yes, I’ll come,’ said the mole, though he had no intention of doing any such thing.

‘You’d better,’ warned the bear as he swaggered off.

The fox, meanwhile, was quite restless. He desperately wanted to put the mole in his place and make him his follower, just like the others. But he was sure the mole would never come to the meeting, so it would never happen.

So when the mole turned up at the next gathering, the fox was very surprised. He decided that the mole must have realized how futile it was to stand against him. He gleefully poked fun at the mole.

‘So the star-nosed clown has decided to please the Oracle, eh?’ the fox said.

‘Hardly,’ said the mole quite calmly. ‘I have come to make an announcement regarding a calamity, and this is the only place where everyone assembles.’

The animals perked up their ears in curiosity, despite their disbelief.

‘There will be an earthquake here, very soon,’ said the mole. ‘I would advise that all of you be on your guard and assemble in the open grasslands as soon as possible.’

‘What!’ snapped the fox. ‘You dare to come and make a prediction when I, the Oracle, am still here?’

'What are you saying, mole?' growled the bear.

'It's the truth,' said the mole.

'Nothing like that is going to happen!' shrieked the fox. 'Do you believe this clown here who can't see a foot ahead of him, or me, your Master?'

'Of course we believe YOU, Master,' said the creatures fervently.

'Go away,' said a few animals curtly to the mole.

'All right,' said the mole, turning away. 'Suit yourselves.'

***

The mole hadn't gone far when the hare stammered nervously, 'I...I think the ground is sh-sh-shaking!'

'You're right!' cried the coyote, as the earth began to move under their feet.

'He was right,' cried the eagle. 'Run!'

The animals lost no time in rushing to the grassland. There was quite a stampede, and they forgot all about the fox who desperately tried to stop them.

The earthquake lasted about five minutes, and when the danger had passed, the mole signalled to everyone to calm down. 'It's fine now,' he said. 'You may all go back and continue your meeting.'

But no one wanted to go back!

'You are our Oracle now,' said the bear, looking downright apologetic.

'Our new Master!' cried the rest.

'Definitely not!' said the mole. 'Stop believing that any one of us has superpowers. Each of us is blessed with certain natural capabilities, and I just happened to use mine. You see my nose that you all make fun of? It's this very nose that lets me sense many things around me, including the vibrations of the earth. As for the fox, he has just been fooling you all these days.'

The bear turned to go back now. 'I'll make mincemeat of that rascal!' he roared.

But he didn't need to.

The fox had fled for his life.

Can the star-nosed mole actually predict earthquakes?

Yes, it can!

The star-nosed mole (*Condylura cristata*) is found in the wet lowland areas of Canada and north-eastern United States. The mole has thick, water-repellent fur, helping it navigate easily both on land and in water. Its thick tail can swell to four times its normal size as it stores fat during winter. It stays underground.

Though blind, the star-nosed mole is adept at catching its prey (mostly earthworms, insects and small aquatic organisms) using its sensitive star-shaped nose, which can detect electric fields around its prey, thus helping it hunt. There are 22 pink, fleshy, tentacle-like projections forming a ring around its snout, acting as a touch organ and giving it a star-like appearance. These projections have on them more than 25,000 minute sensory receptors, called 'Eimer's organs'. Experiments have shown that these sensory receptors are so powerful that they can even sense seismic waves – energy waves that travel through the earth – a result of seismic activity deep underground, thus making the mole well-equipped to detect earthquakes.

6

HOW SANTA GOT RUDOLPH THE REINDEER BACK

It was Christmas time once again. Rudolph, Santa Claus's most favourite reindeer, lay contentedly in his shed at the North Pole, watching the snow fall. Treetops and branches glistened with icicles, and powdery snow covered the rooftops. Some of the snowflakes fell on his shiny red nose – the famous nose – that everyone said had earned him his place as Santa's chief reindeer. It glowed brightly, and Rudolph knew it would shine even brighter on Christmas Eve and guide them all. He felt it was a blessing.

Gradually, Rudolph dozed off, dreaming happy dreams. He loved Christmas, and nothing excited him more than his annual trip across the world on Christmas Eve, pulling Santa's sleigh through the night sky, visiting children as they lay asleep, and leaving presents for them. He looked forward to this one day all through the year.

Just before his eyes closed in slumber, he saw two strangers walk up to Santa's workshop. He had never seen them before. But they didn't look like troublemakers either. Surely, Santa would call him if there was anything urgent? Too lazy to move, Rudolph lay where he was, half-asleep, until another reindeer came rushing in, breathless.

'Rudolph, get up!' said the reindeer, panting. 'Do you know, two men are here, telling Santa that you're too old to draw the sleigh and ought to be replaced!'

'Wha-at?' Rudolph was shocked. It was true that he was many, many years old, but there was nothing 'old' about him. He had always been that way, and was still strong.

'They say you can't see anymore,' the other reindeer said. 'In fact, they say that Santa has so many falls while going around because his reindeer can't see well in the dark winter!'

Now, this was not at all true. The reindeer had always guided Santa around well, leading him safely to rooftops and chimneys and high windows, from where he could get into the houses to leave the Christmas gifts.

'I guess we might all be replaced,' the reindeer continued morosely.

Just then, Santa came in. He looked sad, not at all his usual self. Rudolph looked up inquiringly, hoping whatever he had heard was untrue. But Santa did have bad news.

'I am sorry, my dears,' he said, shaking his head helplessly. 'Those men who came just now say that every year lots of kids don't get their gifts on time. They say it's because you guys can't see in the dark winter. They say your eyes turn blue in the cold, and that blue light doesn't help one see at all. I know you're not at fault, but...they say they will not let me give gifts to any child if I don't replace you all!'

Rudolph was extremely angry. But more than that, he was upset. How could Santa let such a thing happen? Rudolph's eyes filled with tears when he thought of how he would miss seeing the innocent sleeping faces of little children all over the world.

'Who are you replacing us with, Santa?' asked the other reindeer indignantly.

'It's not "who", my dear, it's "what"', said Santa. 'I will be buying a helicopter from those people who came to see me. I will go around in it this time.'

So this was it! Poor Santa was too gullible to even notice the evil design of those upstarts, thought Rudolph. He decided he wouldn't give up his right to draw the sleigh. But then...he didn't want the children to not get their presents because he was stubborn. So, he gave in.

Poor Santa Claus! He wasn't very happy either. But what could he do?

***

The news spread like wildfire. Children came to know that Rudolph wouldn't be coming anymore. They stopped writing to Santa for gifts, because they wanted Santa to take back Rudolph. Santa was in a dilemma. What could he do now?

However, two kids, Maria and Ros, who lived in Norway, decided to do something about it. They approached their father, John, who was a scientist.

'Dad, can't you prove that reindeer can see in the winter darkness too?' they asked him.

Their father thought for a moment. 'Well, of course, they must be able to see quite well, especially since they have been helping Santa out for centuries now. In fact, I'm sure it's not just Rudolph's bright red nose that leads the way!'

'Then prove it, Dad!' they pleaded.

John set to work diligently on it. Day and night he worked, and Christmas Eve drew closer and closer.

On the Eve, just as Santa was about to board the helicopter, John came marching through the snow with Maria and Ros.

'Stop, Santa!' he cried. 'Don't believe those villains!'

Father Christmas stopped in astonishment. Behind John was a huge crowd as well, all there to support Rudolph and the other reindeer!

'Reindeer can see much better in winter than they can ever do in summer!' John declared. 'Their eyes turn blue precisely because their eyes learn to adapt themselves to the low light around – in fact, then they are even more sensitive to light than in the summer, when the reindeer's eyes are yellow!'

The townsfolk had all gathered around the villains who had tried to whisk Santa away in a helicopter. Rudolph, hearing the commotion, came rushing outside. All the children ran and hugged him tight!

'You're back on duty, Rudolph!' cried Maria joyfully.

'We can't do without you!' said Ros.

Santa lost no time in ticking off the men, and asking Rudolph and the other reindeer to draw his sleigh.

And that Christmas was indeed a very, very merry one for Rudolph, the red-nosed reindeer!

What's so special about the reindeer's vision?

When it comes to eyesight in humans or other animals, muscles in our irises contract to dilate our pupils and allow more light into our eyes when we are in the dark. When it's bright again, the irises widen and the pupils shrink. But this happens over a 24-hour period.

Reindeer, on the other hand, cope with three months of constant summer sunlight and three months of perpetual winter darkness, giving rise to a unique phenomenon – reindeer eyes are golden in the summer and blue in the winter. The bit that changes colour is the *tapetum lucidum* or 'cat's eye', a mirrored layer that sits behind the retina in the eye and is made up of collagen, a type of protein whose long fibres are arranged in orderly rows. It helps animals to see in dim conditions by reflecting any light that passes through the retina back onto it, giving its light-detecting cells a second chance to intercept the stray particles of light.

So what happens to the tapetum in reindeer? The harsh Arctic winter forces their pupils to dilate *for months* rather than hours. This continuous strain on the eyes builds up pressure inside it, causing the fluid between the collagen fibres to get squeezed out, so that they become more tightly packed. The spacing of these fibres affects the type of light they reflect. With the usual gaps between them, they reflect yellow wavelengths. When squeezed together during winter, they reflect blue wavelengths, giving the eyes a blue colour.

7

POISON ON THE PLATE

Phials of powders and potions lay in disarray all over the floor. A delicate pair of scales stood on the high table, well out of the reach of the black cat, which lay as silent as death under the small, three-legged stool in the dark, dingy room. The contents of a big iron cauldron bubbled away merrily, its vapours rising into thick white spirals that wafted around, visible in the single shaft of sunlight that beamed in through a hole in the roof.

The cat's whiskers twitched; it didn't seem very happy, but it was quite accustomed to the musty and foul stench that usually filled the room. After all, he was his mistress Locusta's favourite cat, and he was in her favourite room – the one where she made her potions – and poisons.

Locusta walked around the room muttering to herself. 'If only I could find that silly girl who came to assist me,' she grumbled. 'How dare she run away with my stock of Mandrake root powder!' Locusta wasn't very young, but it didn't show on her face. She had managed, with her skill in concocting potions, to find solutions for her ageing skin. Despite her arthritic knees and the slight hump of her back, Locusta still looked beautiful.

Martina, Locusta's rival, another one adept at making poisons, was old, and she looked it. But Canidia, one more infamous poison-maker of Rome, had age on her side – she was still young, but was only third in comparison to Locusta and Martina in terms of skill. It was no wonder then that Locusta, with her beauty and abilities, had managed to have the entire city of Rome trembling at her feet. People came from far and wide to get a potent poison from Locusta to kill their enemies – and she never failed them.

A bell rang somewhere, announcing the entry of a visitor. Locusta turned around, a frown on her face. Visitors were not allowed inside at that hour.

A hooded figure stepped into the room. It was a woman, and her furtive eyes swept around the room as her cloak that covered the rest of her face and form trailed behind her. 'Visitors are not welcome now,' said Locusta haughtily. 'Leave!'

The person did not budge. 'But I am no ordinary visitor, Locusta,' she said, her sharp voice ringing through the room. As she moved forward, her cloak fell off, revealing a beautiful lady dressed in royal silk. Her face showed determination, but her eyes flashed ruthlessness.

Locusta gasped and fell to her knees. 'Your Highness,' she whispered. 'Forgive me.' For the visitor was none other than the empress of Rome, Agrippina, the most powerful woman in the Roman empire at the time.

'What brings you here, Your Highness?' asked Locusta, hurriedly offering a seat to the queen.

'As you know, Locusta,' Agrippina said, refusing the seat with a wave of her hand, 'I have made use of your services before – with satisfactory results.'

'Yes, Your Highness,' mumbled Locusta, a little apprehensive about what was coming. Had she, by mistake, ministered her poisons to a friend or relative of Agrippina's? Had Agrippina come to punish her? Locusta shivered a little at the thought.

Agrippina, however, took no notice of Locusta's pensive state. 'Now it is time for you to concoct the most potent poison ever,' she continued. 'A poison that can be administered without arousing suspicion.'

Locusta heaved a sigh of relief. It looked like Agrippina had come to make use of her services after all. She relaxed a bit. 'For whom is the poison, Your Highness?' she asked.

Agrippina turned her sharp gaze on her. 'It is for Claudius, my husband and the emperor of Rome.'

Locusta was shocked, and at the same time, puzzled. She knew Agrippina was a strong and merciless woman who would go to any lengths to get what she wanted. But this was unexpected.

'Why the emperor?' Locusta enquired. 'If it is to make your son Nero the future emperor of Rome, I would ask you to plot a less risky murder – that of Brittanicus, Claudius's own son.'

'Brittanicus? He is too weak to usurp the kingdom on his own.' Agrippina laughed mirthlessly. 'But, yes, his father is getting a little too fond of him,' she said softly. 'A feeling that is too dangerous to allow.'

'And you want Claudius dead before he chooses his own son as his successor over Nero, his stepson?' Locusta asked.

'Precisely,' snapped Agrippina. 'Get to work now. I want the deadliest poison ever, one that simply cannot fail. You will be rewarded well. And remember, there should be no suspicion. It would be best if he dies only a few days after taking it.'

***

Locusta feverishly worked on the empress' request day and night. She tried out ingredient after ingredient, potion after potion, but she was simply not satisfied. She invented poisons deadlier than any she had made earlier, but all caused instant death.

Locusta was in one of her potion-mixing sessions when her helper Helvia came rushing in. 'Your assistant is dead!' Helvia cried.

'Serves her right,' said Locusta unfeelingly, thinking about the Mandrake root the girl had stolen from her. 'How did it happen?'

'They say she had a mild stomach upset a few days ago. She was all right again for a few days, and suddenly, she fell ill and died.'

Locusta was suddenly interested. 'How could that be? She was quite healthy!'

'Her sister told me,' whispered the girl, 'that she ate some greenish-white mushrooms that she found deep in the forest.'

Locusta sighed. She had hoped to find some new poison that no one knew about. But if the dead girl's

sister had already told Helvia, then she must have told others as well.

'But I'm the only one she told this to, you see,' said Helvia proudly. 'It's our secret.'

'Why?' asked Locusta.

'Because if she tells others, they'd ask her why her sister went into the forest at all. No one knows that that's where she used to hide the things she stole from others!'

That very night, Locusta made a trip to the forest and collected the deadly death cap mushrooms.

***

Claudius, the Roman emperor and the great-great-grandnephew of Julius Caesar, sat down to his dinner. His taster, Halotus, stood beside him at the table, a bit apprehensively. A short distance away, out of Claudius's sight, stood Agrippina, watching both of them.

'So no poison in my food today, eh?' Claudius joked. 'You're sure that none of my wives want me killed today?' He laughed bitterly, thinking of his daily fights with Agrippina.

'I have already tasted the food, Your Highness,' said Halotus, a slight tremor to his voice.

Claudius ate his meal, talking merrily to Halotus, unaware that the poison from the death cap mushrooms was already mixed in his meal.

That night, he slept soundly.

The next morning, the royal physician was called to the emperor's bedside to treat him for severe diarrhoea and cramps. The physician assured him of a speedy recovery, while taking a bag of gold from the queen on the sly. Claudius confidently gave a haughty smile to his detractors, which included Agrippina, as he returned to normalcy that night.

Agrippina did not react. She smiled to herself.

Ten days later, as Claudius lay in his grave, her son Nero was crowned king.

What are death cap mushrooms?

The death cap mushroom is basically a fungus, which is responsible for the most mushroom poisonings in the world. Scientifically named *Amanita phalloides*, it is one of the most lethal mushrooms. Found throughout Europe, the mycelia (the thin network of fungal filaments) of the fungus fuses with the roots of broad-leaved trees like chestnut and oak for nutrient exchange. This kind of a relationship is called a '*mycorrhizal* [say *my-co-rye-zal*] relationship'.

These toxic mushrooms look a lot like other edible species, leading to many cases of accidental poisoning. They have greenish- or yellowish-white caps, which are often sticky to touch.

Anyone who eats a death cap mushroom will not show any symptoms for 10–14 hours, after which they will suffer from vomiting, diarrhoea and cramps, which disappear in a while. After 3–4 days, the patient suffers a kidney or liver failure and dies within 5–10 days of ingesting the mushroom. The Roman emperor Claudius is said to have been poisoned with the death cap mushroom by his wife, who wanted to make Nero the next ruler of Rome.

The chief toxic component of the mushroom is Alpha-amanitin, which along with Beta-amanitin, slows down the making of protein in body cells. The main organ affected is the liver, because it is the first organ that the toxin encounters after absorption in the digestive tract.

8

THE SILK ROUTE TO AHIMSA

'Daddy, are we there?' Reshmi asked for the umpteenth time.

Her dad laughed. 'Patience, Reshmi,' he said, 'I told you it would take another hour!'

Reshmi smiled and hugged herself, unable to contain her excitement. It was her ninth birthday, and she was sitting in the car, waiting for her birthday surprise. Reshmi looked pretty in her brand-new dress – a beautiful blue long skirt and blouse made of fine silk.

But many of Reshmi's dresses were silk anyway, whether it was her birthday or not! Being the only daughter of well-to-do parents, Reshmi had always been pampered with the best of things. Her parents had named her 'Reshmi' after the Hindi word for silk – '*resham*'. Her doting parents also loved to dress her up in rich silks on every special occasion and told her they had named her so after the fine fabric that implied royalty and elegance.

And, true to her name, Reshmi was as soft as silk in the way she spoke and in everything she did. She was high-spirited, but never impolite or hurtful to anyone. Reshmi herself liked wearing silk, and the soft material that came in various colours and patterns caught her fancy. What she prized most among her possessions, in her own words, was what she was called – silk.

That birthday, her father had promised her a surprise. Reshmi wasn't sure what it was, but she secretly hoped it was a visit to her grandfather's house. Reshmi had never been there, though her grandpa had come to visit her several times. Her dad wouldn't tell her where they were going; nor would her mother, the cook or the house help, who all seemed to be in on the secret. In the end, Reshmi had to sit back in the car quietly, waiting to reach the surprise destination.

Almost two hours later, the car drove up into the grounds of a large country cottage. Reshmi gaped in wonder at the new surroundings, full of greenery, and the quaint old house, both in stark contrast to her city home. She got out of the car excitedly when the door of the cottage was opened by her grandfather.

'Dadaji!!' she cried, rushing into his arms. She was very fond of her grandfather and missed him, because he hardly ever stayed with them more than a week in the city. He always said he 'had work to do' in the village.

Her grandfather was equally delighted to see her. He took her around the house, showing her every nook and cranny.

'So this was the surprise you planned for me!' Reshmi said to her father, who was standing by and watching the grandfather–granddaughter pair at play.

'Well, yes, but there was something else that I actually meant to show you!' replied her father, his eyes shining merrily.

'Aah, yes,' said her grandfather. 'We thought we would show you how your most favourite thing – silk – is made.'

Reshmi was surprised. For all her obsession with silk, she had never given a thought to how it was made. She had taken it for granted that silk was bought at shops...

'Do you know that your grandfather has a silk production unit right here?' asked her father. "

Reshmi looked at her grandfather in awe. 'Dadaji, you never told me!' she said. 'Do you have huge machines and a big industrial building here to produce silk?

Her grandfather laughed. 'Come with me,' he said, and led her towards the backyard. He first took her to a loom, where numerous weavers were at work. 'Here, they weave the silk thread into silk cloth, in different colours and patterns that you're so fond of,' he explained.

'But where does the silk thread come from?' Reshmi asked him.

Her grandfather took her to a huge room full of baskets and trays stacked one on top of another. There was a continuous pitter-pattering sound, as if huge raindrops were falling on the roof.

'Brrr...it's quite cold in here, Dadaji,' said Reshmi. 'And what's that strange sound?'

'Open one of these baskets and you'll see,' said her grandfather. Reshmi lifted the cover off one to find it full of green leaves and greyish-white worms munching away on the leaves. She leaped back in shock. 'Worms!' she cried.

'Not just worms, my dear,' said her father, '*silk*worms.'

'Here are your silk producers,' said her grandfather. 'These silkworms are the larvae, or the caterpillars of the silk moth. From the time they hatch, they feed voraciously on the leaves of mulberry trees.'

'And once they have had their fill,' her father continued, 'they prepare themselves for a long nap all wrapped up in a cocoon, during which time their bodies change to become moths.'

'Ooh... just like the butterfly!' said Reshmi. 'But where does the silk come from?'

Her grandfather led her to a different room, where there were several workers handling what looked like small white balls. 'Those are the silkworm cocoons,' he said. 'The silkworms produce the silk fibre from their saliva, from certain glands in their body, and wind this fibre round and round themselves several times, to make the cocoon.'

'But we have saliva too,' insisted Reshmi. 'How come it doesn't form strong fibres like silk?'

'Raw silk made by these worms is made of two proteins – fibroin and sericin,' said her father. 'The fibroin is like a strong thread. The sericin is a gum-like protein that binds two strands of fibroin together.'

Her grandfather then showed Reshmi how the workers extracted the silk thread from the cocoons. 'Just before the moth emerges, the cocoons are steamed to kill the half-grown moth inside, and then dipped in boiling water. That allows the silk thread to come loose from the cocoon...which is then spun onto a reel.'

Reshmi stood rooted to the spot. She had enjoyed the entire experience till she realized that the moths in the cocoons were killed to produce silk. Her eyes filled with tears as she saw hundreds of cocoons being steamed. Before her father could stop her, she ran out, all the way to the car. She wouldn't stay there a minute longer.

Her father tried to pacify her, but she wouldn't listen. Finally, he gave up and drove her back home. As soon as she reached home, she took out all the silk clothes from her wardrobe. 'I won't wear silk anymore,' she announced. 'Had I known that silk is made by killing so many harmless creatures, I would never have worn it!'

***

Months passed, and nothing could make Reshmi change her mind.

Then one day, a parcel arrived from her grandfather, along with a letter.

My dear Reshmi,

I never thought how terrible it was to kill so many moths to make silk, till you made me think of it. Just for your sake, I have now started making silk differently – without harming the cocoons. We let the worms come out and fly away, and then extract the silk from the cocoons. We call it 'Ahimsa' silk, or 'non-violent' silk. Here's your first dress made from this 'peaceful' silk – hope you like it.

–Love, Dadaji

Reshmi opened the parcel to find a gorgeous red silk dress. It was not as fine to touch as the silk she was used to, but she held it close to herself, delighted that no worms were killed for it.

Can silk really be made without killing silkworms?

Yes, it can.

The rearing of silkworms to produce silk is called **sericulture**, a practice that originated in China. The silkworms or rather the larvae of the silk moth (*Bombyx mori*) are used for making silk commercially. The female silk moth lays around 300 eggs at a time on the leaves of the mulberry plant, and when they hatch, the silkworms feed on the same leaves. The worms moult or shed their skin four times, after which they enter the pupal stage, where they spin a cocoon. It is this cocoon made of a continuous thread of raw silk, around 300–900 metres long, which is spun from the glands of the worm.

The strength and elasticity of the silk thread comes from the proteins fibroin and sericin present in the silk thread. While fibroin is the thread-like component, sericin is the gum that holds the threads together. Once the worm has metamorphosed into an adult moth, it breaks out of the cocoon.

In sericulture, moths are not allowed to break out of the cocoon as this breaks the silk thread, making it commercially useless. Hence, the cocoons are steamed or baked to kill the half-developed moths inside and then dipped in boiling water to extract the silk thread.

Mahatma Gandhi was highly critical of silk production because of this very reason, and instead supported the production of Eri silk or Ahimsa silk. This involves obtaining silk from cocoons of wild or semi-domesticated moths, where the moth is allowed to break out of one end of the cocoon, which is then used for silk extraction. A new technique involves placing larvae on a pedestal where they spin silk which winds around the stand but does not form a cocoon. Yet, the larvae metamorphose into adults.

9

THE CARDINAL'S NATURAL COSMETICS

Alex looked out of the window. The sun was already high up in the sky. A pair of red cardinal birds sat on a post right opposite their house. He knew his ornithologist father would be watching the birds carefully.

'Why can't I be like them?' thought Alex wistfully. *Free and happy*, he thought. *They don't have to go to school. They don't have to take these stupid baths!*

He was late for school as usual, but he didn't care. He could hear his mother calling him from the kitchen, but he didn't bother to answer. He knew what would happen if he went to her then. She would surely push him into the shower and make him take a bath! He hated taking baths. Why did people have to take a bath every day?

His elder sister, Alice, who was already a teenager, was just the opposite. She spent a lot of time in front of the bathroom mirror (at least, according to Alex), bought a lot of cosmetics, and didn't mind taking several showers a day. 'It helps clear my pores,' she told Alex solemnly when he asked her why she had a minimum of five baths every day. 'I hate these pimples!'

Alex's mother called again from the kitchen. He quickly pulled on a T-shirt and his favourite blue jeans, and ran his fingers through his hair to smooth them down. He could hear his father talking to someone on the phone in his room. Alice's hairdryer buzzed in her room. There seemed to be enough noise around to cover his tracks. Alex quietly tiptoed out into the hall. He opened the big glass windows and stepped out into the lawn, carrying his school bag and shoes in his hand. As soon as he was out, he quickly put on his shoes and ran across the lawns and right out of the gate.

'Alex, come back!' yelled his mother when she spotted him from the kitchen window. 'What about breakfast?'

Alex ran without waiting to look back. He sprinted all the way to school. On the way he snatched a sandwich from Rodney, his friend, who was slowly walking towards the school gate.

'Hey! ' Rodney cried.

'Small sacrifice for friendship,' said Alex good-naturedly to his friend. 'I'm sure you ate at home. '

'That I did,' said Rodney in a mournful tone. 'And I have one more sandwich in my bag.' They walked into the school just as the bell rang.

Alex sank into his seat in class. His classmate, Janet, who sat next to him in class, wrinkled her nose as he came close. 'Don't sit next to me, Alex,' she hissed at him. 'You smell like a pig! '

Alex merely raised an eyebrow and leaned back in the chair.

Janet made a face at him and moved away to an empty seat. She whispered something to the girl sitting next to her. Alex didn't care.

The first two hours passed without incident. The next class was gym class. Alex had forgotten his gym clothes in the hurry. He rummaged in his locker and found an unwashed set that had been worn several times. 'I guess this should do for today,' Alex told himself.

He walked into the class confidently, only to be stopped at the door by the gym teacher. 'You're not walking into my class this way, mister,' he said. 'You look like you haven't had a wash in years! Get a fresh set of clothes and then perhaps I'll let you in!'

Alex came out quietly, knowing he couldn't argue.

He wandered around the school grounds, peeping into the other classes. He saw Alice sitting in the last bench in her class. He saw her rummaging in her bag. She smoothened her foundation and reapplied lipstick, looking into her small hand-held mirror. The teacher didn't seem to notice. Next, Alice took out a perfume and sprayed herself with it. Alex smirked. This was fascinating to watch. Just then the teacher called Alice, who stood up in a hurry.

But before he could hear what the commotion was about, he found himself being pulled up by the scruff of his neck. 'Why are you out here?' came a booming voice. Alex found himself face to face with the school principal. 'Are you really a student of this school?' he asked, peering closely at Alex. 'You look more like a vagabond.'

Alex found himself being dragged to the principal's office. There was no chance of getting away. 'I'm calling your parents right now,' the principal said sternly, glaring at Alex. 'Never have I seen such an untidy student in my life. Haven't you learnt anything about personal hygiene? How could you—'

A knock came at the door. A teacher came inside, visibly furious. And right behind her, walked in, shamefaced – Alice!

'Alice spent all the money that the class collected this year for charity,' the teacher said.

'How irresponsible!' exclaimed the principal. 'What did you spend it on?'

'Uh, she says she spent it on expensive soaps and shampoos,' said the teacher. 'She was planning to replace it...'

Alice nodded, her head bowed.

The principal still looked incredulous. 'But that was a huge amount!' he said. 'I can't believe you spent it all only on cosmetics!'

She isn't lying,' spoke up Alex. 'She has always been like that, over obsessed with cosmetics and cleanliness and—'

The principal glared at Alex. 'And *you* don't even know what soap is, I suppose?'

***

That day the principal gave a long lecture to Alex's parents, who in turn gave an equally serious one to Alice and Alex. Neither Alex nor Alice had the nerve to meet their parents' eyes, and they stood with their heads hung.

'Maintaining personal hygiene is a must,' said Alex's dad to him. 'I know you hate taking baths, but do you know that even animals make sure they're clean? See those red cardinals out there? Those birds keep themselves clean by covering themselves in ants. They crush them to release an acid so that their feathers are all clean and free from mites. Learn from them!' he shouted at Alex before turning to Alice.

'Alice, you need to learn from the cardinals too. They don't go looking for the biggest or the most exotic ants to rub on themselves. They make do with the ants around. I hope you understand you needn't spend on cosmetics so much anymore!'

Do the red cardinals really use ants as their cosmetics?

Yes, they do!

Red cardinals are seed-eating birds found in North and South America. They display a specific bird behaviour called 'anting', during which they rub insects, usually ants, on their feathers and skin. The bird may pick up the insects in its beak and rub them on its body, or the bird may lie in an area with a large number of insects and have a dry 'ant' bath! The insects, when crushed, secrete certain chemicals like formic acid, which protect the birds from other insects, mites, and fungal and bacterial infections. Anting could also help make the insects edible by removing the distasteful acid, or could supplement the bird's own natural oil that is secreted for preening and grooming. Instead of ants, birds may also use millipedes! More than 200 species of birds are known to display this phenomenon. In addition, other animals such as squirrels and pangolins may also exhibit anting-type behaviour.

10

WHO OWNS THE RIVER?

It was still dark outside, but Chang was already out with his fishing net. He pushed out his little boat into the River Yangtze, and it rocked gently on the waves. He said a silent prayer to his dead father's soul, as he slipped into the boat, that he should get a good catch that day. His father had been a fisherman too. He thought wistfully of his younger brother Liu, who no longer stayed with him. Liu had refused his father's request to become a fisherman and gone to Shanghai to take up a job.

Chang sighed and set about his work. He belonged to a family that followed traditional fishing methods. He didn't want a catch that provided him more than he needed; he wanted just enough to fulfil his needs for that day. But huge fishing trawlers had begun to roam the rivers of the Yangtze now, monsters that used electronic and mechanical devices to catch fish. The 'fishing trawls' – large nets that were pulled along the bottom of the river – hauled in lots of fish of all kinds. They were owned by big commercial fishing companies that sought to make profits and nothing else.

The trawlers were a danger to small-time fishermen like Chang, who had to go fishing earlier than usual to get his share. As he threw his net into the black waters, Chang wondered how he would carry on his work with the fishing companies growing in strength. He would probably end up having to find work on those trawlers, he mused.

As Chang pulled in his net, he was delighted to find big mandarin fish, sturgeons and carp among his catch. But his net was still heavy. Wondering what he had caught, he pulled it in further. He was shocked to find a baiji – the whitefin dolphin that lived in their river – trapped in his net!

'What have I done?' thought Chang. 'Oh, the poor gentle creature! I must free it at once!' The baiji was considered the Goddess of the Yangtze, which made Chang feel twice as guilty. He hurriedly tried to disentangle his nets and free the dolphin, but the more he tried, the knottier they got, for his hands were trembling with trepidation. The dolphin lay motionless, but looked at him with its small mournful eyes, breathing heavily.

At last, Chang cut open his net and gently pushed the dolphin out. The dolphin swam out into the water, and jumped a small loop in the air, as though thanking

him for letting it go. Chang sat down, tired. Some of the other fish he had caught escaped too, and Chang was left with a very small catch. His only good net was spoilt as well. He sat there, lost in thought about what he would do next. Maybe he could borrow some money from the local moneylender to buy a new fishing net.

A horn sounded from a steamboat nearby, snapping Chang out of his reverie. What a busy place the river was becoming, he wondered. He watched as a fishing trawler made its way down the river. What if the trawler caught the dolphin he had just freed, thought Chang apprehensively. Holding the spoilt fishing net in his hands, he made his way back home, promising himself that come what may, he would not work for the commercial fishing companies.

***

Years passed, and Chang remained the poor fisherman he was. His business went from bad to worse. The river was no longer the plentiful source of food, but a decaying water body that was being used indiscriminately for its resources, and also a busy waterway.

Their village was no longer a peaceful haven, but a busy, polluted commercial town with lots of activity and commotion all through the day and night. They now had electricity and big industries that provided employment to thousands of people. Chang could not adapt to the change, and he felt hopeless about the future. One day, however, something happened to lift his spirits. It was a letter from Liu. After all those years! Liu was finally coming back home!

When Liu arrived, he was hardly recognizable. City life had changed him, and he looked sophisticated in his urban clothes, while Chang remained the poor villager. Liu's talk, his mannerisms, had all changed. 'Going to Shanghai was the best decision of my life, brother,' he told Chang gleefully. 'I know that wasn't what our poor father had wanted from me, but...'

'That's all right, brother,' said Chang, who was more than overjoyed to see his sibling again. On the way home, he took Liu in his boat down the river to relive their old memories.

'Is that a baiji there?' exclaimed Liu suddenly. 'It's been ages since I have seen one. Can we row closer there?'

'There are no more whitefin dolphins left in the river, brother,' said Chang sadly. 'That may not be a baiji.'

'Oh,' said Liu, and shrugged.

They came back home for lunch, a simple meal prepared by Chang. Liu wrinkled his nose at the small hut that had stood from their father's time. 'What's this, brother? Why are you staying in this old, broken-down hut when all around you better houses with electricity have come up?'

Chang only gave a wan smile. 'What work do you do there, brother?' he asked, changing the subject. 'You seem to have done very well for yourself!'

'Oh, haven't you heard of the dams we built on the river?' asked Liu proudly. 'I am one of those who were involved in it from the very beginning. I started off very small, but now I am in a high position. All this prosperity that you see in our village is because of our work. The dams we built harness water to generate electricity, which is very cheap! That's why everyone here is able to afford it. I also have a stake in some of these commercial fishing companies.'

'I thought you hadn't wanted to be a fisherman at all, Liu, but it looks like you have become one after all, and on a much larger scale than me or Father,' said Chang quietly.

Liu scowled. 'Oh, I'm not doing any fishing myself, am I?' he asked defensively. 'I just get a share of the profits from it.'

'A very good share, I must say,' said Chang silently eyeing Liu's get-up and his bulging pockets. 'But what about the river itself? Did you think about how it has been damaged by your work? You asked me about the baijis. Do you realize that not a single one is left now?'

'So?' asked Liu, with a sneer. 'Do the baijis own the river and we can't use it? Haven't you been using the river too, Chang, by being a fisherman? Is the harm done only when I do something?'

'I have never taken more than what I need,' replied Chang. 'Nor did Father. And we never polluted the river in the ways you have, or disturbed the life of the creatures in the river to this extent.'

Liu didn't have an answer. He changed the subject, spoke about the weather, and about his wife and kids back in Shanghai. As he was about to leave, he invited Chang to visit him at Shanghai. 'And you should break down this hut and build a proper house,' he told his poor brother. 'How can I bring my family here to this poor shelter?'

'Why don't you rebuild this yourself?' said Chang, smiling. 'I don't have the money.'

Liu frowned. 'Why should I? You own this hut, not me! I don't own it.'

Chang laughed. 'Did you own the river then, that you could exploit it so much?'

Did humans destroy the river ecosystem of the River Yangtze in China?

Yes, they did!

The baiji (*Lipotes vexillifer*) or the Yangtze river dolphin of China, also called the whitefin dolphin, was the first dolphin to be declared 'extinct' in current times. Within a few decades of rapid industrialization and the setting up of hydroelectric projects on the river, the population of the baiji went from 6,000 in the 1950s to zero in the 2000s. The dolphins were sometimes caught in fishing nets, or struck by boats and steamers, or killed by the pollutants and effluents released by the industries surrounding the Yangtze. The baiji was declared extinct in December 2006 after an extensive survey, with the causes being entirely man-made.

The baiji, like all other dolphins, was a mammal, and hence breathed through its lungs. Its vision was poor, and hence it relied mainly on sonar (use of sound waves) for navigation. It was the only living representative of the family *Lipotidae*, and evolutionarily distinct. Pale blue to grey on the dorsal (back) side, and white on the ventral (belly) side, it had a dorsal fin that resembled a light-coloured flag when the dolphin swam just below the surface of the murky river waters, earning it its name – 'whitefin'.

11

THE MYSTERIOUS ROOM IN MRS CELL'S HOUSE

Mrs Cell was proud of her house. It would be an exaggeration to say that she lived in a palace, or a bungalow that had beautiful statues and pools adorning it; but to stick to the truth, Mrs Cell's house was a very neat and compact one. Just the right size and the right shape. She had a strong double-layered wall all around, that made her feel even more smug about it. Her highly talented daughters made her house a lively place, and she thought the wall a good idea to keep them safe. They had very complicated names – not at all as short and sweet as Cell – and Mrs Cell would talk of their achievements to anyone she met.

'Yes, my Mitochondria, you see – she was the one who gave us all the energy to keep going – such a ghastly incident, you know. We had quite a shock, but poor thing, she kept us motivated—'

Or, it would be something like this: 'Oh yes, Nucleus is my eldest daughter, the smartest of the whole lot – no one can match her brains, why, she has so much of knowledge stored—'

On the whole, Mrs Cell loved to brag, so she was usually avoided at parties, for she would start off on her wonderful house and her even more amazing daughters. Everyone was tired of it.

But Mrs Cell had a secret. Deep within her home was a locked room. No one knew about it, except she and her daughters. When Mitochondria and Ribosome questioned their mother about it, she snapped at them. 'None of your business!' she said sharply. 'If you want to stay alive, stay away from that room!' And the children would slink away.

Sometimes, some of them saw Mrs Cell quietly putting something wrapped in plastic bags into the room, but she wouldn't let anyone near her. The younger ones whispered among themselves, hazarding guesses at what might be in the secret room. 'I'm sure Mum's got a treasure hidden away there,' said Ribosome, one of the younger kids. 'She just doesn't want to show us, and she's probably dumping wads of cash there from time to time.'

'Or maybe it's a monster,' said tall and lanky Endoplasmic Reticulum (called Endo for short), trembling. 'Maybe she feeds the monster every day.' It was usually Endo who gave her mother the plastic bags for the 'secret' work, and she had seen her putting in a

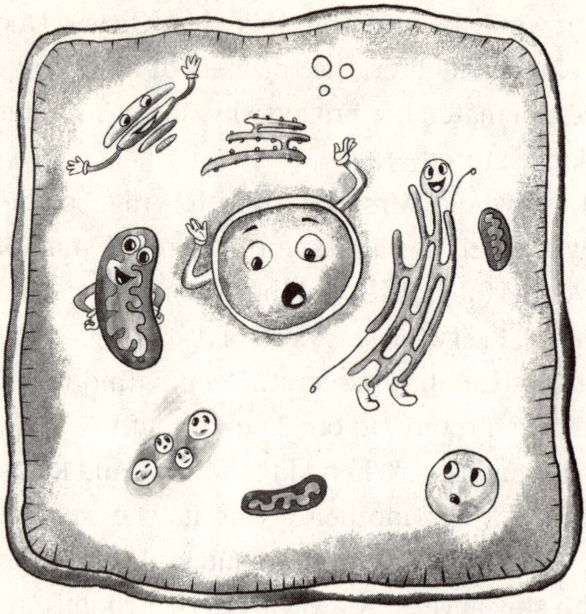

few food items sometimes. She was convinced that her mother kept a pet monster, and had nightmares about the secret room.

They tried asking Nucleus, who was the eldest, as she seemed to have an inkling of what was in the secret room. But Nucleus would take on a pompous attitude and shoo them away. 'Mother knows what she's doing,' she would say. 'Now off with you, or I'll complain to Mother about you nosy parkers!'

So the door remained locked, and the room remained a mystery. As time passed, the locked room became a part of their lives that they took no notice of.

***

Now Mrs Cell had quite a lavish lifestyle, for she had lots of money in the bank, and all she ever did was spend it. She never bothered to keep a check on her accounts, and as long as she had money flowing in, she did not feel the need to worry, for it got them all the food and clothes and other things they needed. She often bought things in excess – sometimes she used them, sometimes she didn't – and stored the remaining or left them lying about the house.

The, one day, tragedy struck. Mrs Cell discovered that she had no more money flowing in from the bank. Her account was empty!

Gloom descended on the house. Mrs Cell was grumpy and irritable, and everyone else was upset. Nucleus gave lectures on the importance of saving and the economic use of resources, while Mitochondria tried to cheer everyone up. But things went from bad to worse, and soon they were all at the point of starvation.

That day, Mrs Cell gathered all her daughters. 'It is time to open the locked room,' she announced gravely. 'I tried not to...but now there is no other way.'

'Look, I was right,' whispered Ribosome to a scared and whimpering Endo. 'She's kept a treasure there and now she's going to use it.'

Mrs Cell unlocked the door and the girls peered in. It was pitch dark inside. 'Come on,' shouted Mrs Cell without stepping in. 'Wake up! You're needed!'

It was Endo's turn to whisper now. 'There, I told you, it's a monster! Who speaks to wads of cash like that?'

They heard footsteps as someone came closer to the door. There appeared another girl just like them, but dishevelled and untidy. A strange smell hung about her, and the others wrinkled their noses. Mitochondria scrunched up her face, trying to hide her disgust (but failing to do so), while Nucleus looked at her with distaste. And then, Mrs Cell announced a most astonishing thing. 'This is also my daughter – that is, your sister – Lysosome.'

Everyone gasped in shock, while Lysosome herself grinned at them all innocently. How could that be? The look of dismay on Nucleus's face revealed that she too had not known anything about it.

'But...but...Mother, how could you do such a thing? How could you lock her up like that? She is one of us!'

Mrs Cell looked pained and disgusted at the same time. 'I shouldn't have, but...but...how could I tell everyone that Lysosome...recycles garbage?'

Nucleus had had enough. 'So you thought of her only now, when you need her to recycle all the junk we have here, so that we don't starve!' Nucleus raged. 'Lysosome will not stay locked anymore, Mother. She is our saviour! I will not let you hide her away!'

'We won't, we won't,' joined in the others.

Mrs Cell was quite ashamed. 'I am sorry, Lysosome, I treated you very badly,' she said. 'Will you help us now?'

Lysosome nodded, not in the least offended.

'Get that bag of rotten onions,' Nucleus called. Lysosome carefully separated the completely rotten ones from the ones that could still be used. She did the same with the potatoes and the tomatoes and even the old clothes – repairing some, cutting bits and pieces from older dresses to make a new dress and so on.

And within no time, Lysosome managed to recycle all the extra junk and food that Mrs Cell had hoarded up here and there, making things better for them, and they survived for days. And then, Mrs Cell got news that she still had an account with money in it, so life was soon back to normal for them. And Mrs Cell's house was beautiful again, with Lysosome getting an equally important place in her home as her sisters, as she deserved.

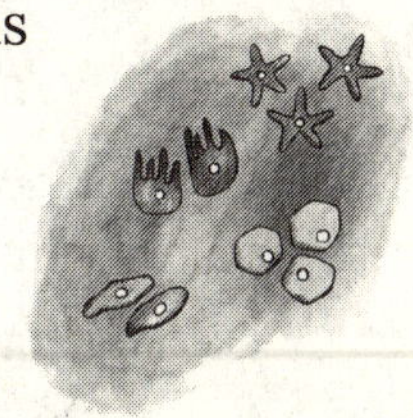

Does the lysosome really play such an important role in a cell?

Yes, it does!

The 2016 Nobel Prize in Physiology or Medicine went to Japanese cell biologist Yoshinori Ohsumi for his discovery of how 'autophagy' – a cellular process – works. Autophagy is a fundamental mechanism for breaking down and recycling cellular components. The word is of Greek origin, in which *auto* means 'self' and *phagein* means 'to eat', thus translating as 'self-eating'.

The cell can destroy its own contents by enclosing it in membranes, forming tiny 'blister'-like vesicles that are transported to a recycling compartment, called the *lysosome*, for degradation. The lysosome contains enzymes that can break down the contents transported to it, whether they be carbohydrates, or proteins, or fats. While the lysosome is present in higher animals and mammalian cells, in plants, the 'vacuole' carries out the functions of the lysosome.

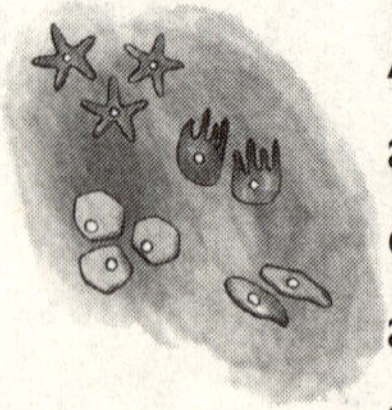

The term 'autophagy' was coined by Christian de Duve, the Belgian scientist who also discovered the lysosome. Autophagy occurs in a cell in certain circumstances – such as when it is subjected to starvation, or when it needs extra energy, or is infected by another organism. Sometimes autophagy can occur even during periods of normalcy as part of the cell's general housekeeping activities.

Yoshinori Ohsumi used baker's yeast to identify the genes that directed the process of autophagy and discovered that several proteins and protein complexes were involved in the process. His findings help us understand the adaptation to starvation or response to infection. Defects in the autophagy process have been found to play a role in causing Parkinson's disease and Type-2 diabetes.

12

A SUNNY JOURNEY ACROSS THE WORLD

It was the 12th century CE. The sun was beating down severely, and Peru was melting in the summer heat. Acclacuna, the chief priestess of the Incas, adjusted her headdress again. The sunflowers that made it up looked resplendent. But they weren't sitting quite firmly on her head.

'Chuki!' she called out impatiently. 'Chuki, where are you?'

Chuki, the peasant girl, who was also Acclacuna's personal attendant, came rushing in. She was quite scared of the priestess, who could be very severe.

'It is almost time for me to offer worship to Inti,' she said, in a grave, priestly tone. Inti was the Sun God, whom the Incas worshipped. As the Priestess to the Sun, Acclacuna held an important position among the Incas. The sunflowers on her head were considered sacred and were meant to honour the Sun God.

'The sunflowers have not been fixed properly,' Acclacuna continued, as a silent Chuki stood there with her head bowed and hands folded. 'Fix them as they should be placed.'

Chuki timidly stepped forward and started rearranging the flowers on the priestess' head. The sunflowers themselves were quite happy to have been chosen for such an important reason. *What a privilege!* they thought.

But Acclacuna was getting impatient. 'It is time for the ceremony. It is time to appease the Sun God. And if we don't—' she said sharply, leaving the rest of the sentence unsaid, for effect. 'Do it quickly, or the fire of heaven will strike you down!'

Chuki trembled in fear and tried to hurry. At last, it was done.

Acclacuna walked away, and Chuki rushed back to perform her other duties. But unfortunately for Chuki, one of the sunflowers fell and Chuki stamped on it in her hurry to go. She did not notice it at all. But when Acclacuna came back, she saw the trampled sunflower lying on the floor.

'May the curse of the Sun God be upon you!' she screamed in fury. And poor Chuki was punished for her mistake.

***

Centuries passed. The sunflowers bloomed day after day in the Americas alone, turning up their lovely faces to the sun.

If the natives of South America used sunflowers for worship, the natives of North America were eating them. The sunflower seeds were ground to make a fine powder, which was then mixed with flour to make bread.

But the year 1532 brought bad news from across the oceans. The Spaniards invaded Peru, and there was a war. The Incas, who had never known gunfire or cannon, tasted defeat easily, despite the Spanish army being small in size. Worse, they were infected by smallpox, a killer disease, for the first time, and many of the Incas died of the infection.

'It is the wrath of the gods!' screamed the priests and priestesses of the sun, but even they could do nothing as big boils covered the bodies of the indigenous people and they died a painful death. The Spaniards had, of course, been exposed to the disease earlier and so did not suffer as much.

Pizarro, the Spanish explorer who had led the conquest, was satisfied with his work. He was even happier when he saw the vast fields of sunflowers – and some of the sunflower seeds made it to his pocket, and those of some other Spaniards, who took them back to Spain.

And so the sunflowers travelled to Europe. It was colder there, but they grew well nonetheless. The

sunflower became an exotic ornamental plant, which was then used by the Europeans for decoration and beauty. Holland now had not just tulip fields but also sunflowers shining golden yellow. And there the sunflowers stayed for another two centuries.

The tsar of Russia, Peter the Great, was touring Holland when he chanced upon the sunflowers. 'What beautiful flowers!' he commented.

The sunflowers made for a magnificent sight, with their stalks upright and their lovely long yellow petals spread all around in geometric precision.

The tsar was so impressed that he took some sunflower seeds back home with him, and asked his gardeners to plant them around. And soon, Russia had sunflowers, while of course the Russians had no idea about the plant. They stared in wonder at the sunflowers, but didn't know of what use it could be to them, until it was time for Lent.

Now Lent was a six-week period of fasting before Easter, and all Christians were expected to give up certain luxuries during this time, and that included some types of food. The Church took great pains to specify exactly which foods were prohibited during this time, and that included lard, butter and oil as well! Just then, the people realized the (possibly unintentional) kindness of Peter the Great.

'Hey, we can use sunflower oil!' they said joyfully, because the Church had completely forgotten about including sunflowers in its list.

Soon sunflowers became a hit with the Russians. By 1830, sunflowers were being grown on large scale for the production of oil. And what was more, they had developed vastly improved varieties of sunflowers, which could produce a large amount of oil.

By now, the sunflower was no longer the simple plant that bloomed in Peru. From its humble beginnings in the South and North America, it had gone all the way to Europe! Not only had it grown to adapt to different climates in various countries, but was of a much superior quality as well, as years of cultivation and selective breeding had ensured that the best varieties thrived.

Russians who started migrating to America now took sunflower seeds with them, thus introducing the improved varieties back in its homeland.

And that was how the sunflower enjoyed a sunny trip across the world and back!

Did sunflowers really go across the world?

Yes, they did!

The common sunflower or *Helianthus annuus*, is a large annual herb that is grown as a crop for its edible oil and seeds. The plant was first domesticated in the Americas. Sunflower cultivation dates back as far as 3000 BCE in Arizona and New Mexico, and the flower was considered sacred by the Incas of Peru, as it represented the Sun God.

In the late 16th century, after the Spanish conquest of Peru, the sunflower was brought to Europe and called the 'Indian Sun' or the 'Golden Flower of Peru'. It was in England where sunflower oil was first marketed in 1716. Russia's tsar, Peter the Great, was also responsible for starting their cultivation in Russia.

By 1830, the manufacture of sunflower oil was done on a commercial scale. The Russian Orthodox Church increased its popularity when it forbade most oil foods from being consumed during Lent, except oil made from sunflowers. By the early 19th century, Russian farmers were growing sunflowers on over 2 million acres of land.

V.S. Pustovoit, a Russian scientist, was instrumental in developing high-yielding varieties of sunflower, which were then brought back to America. Being rich in healthy omega-6 and omega-9 fats, unsaturated fats and vitamin E, sunflower oil soon started becoming a favourite in England and European countries to control cholesterol, a kind of fat found in body cells.

13

IT TAKES A TEAM TO TANGO

'I'm hungry,' remarked the biggest one in the group.

'Yes, yes, so are we,' said the irritable one.

'What do you think we are doing, playing marbles?' said the sarcastic one.

'Oh, give him a break,' said the 'good' one.

'You guys are moving too fast,' remarked the lazy one.

'Can't be avoided,' said the serious one. 'You want to move at all, you have to do it in a pack.'

They were all elongated rod-shaped creatures – just single bacterial cells, in fact – moving together on a lumpy field. One had to glide over the other to move ahead – but this was a fine arrangement, for a single bacterium could never move if it were on its own. The group was always a mix of characters – there was a serious, bossy cell; a kind and smiling one; some irritable and some lazy, but they kept together despite the differences.

'Look...food ahead!' cried the biggest cell, which was always hungry for food. The call was enough for the rest of the group.

'Full charge on!' cried the leader, the serious, bossy one, and they hurriedly stumbled – or glided – over each other to get at the 'food'.

The food happened to be a lump of another set of bacterial cells. 'They seem to have been placed there for our benefit,' frowned the leader. 'Are we walking into a trap?'

'Food is good, food is good,' chanted the biggest one, rushing onwards, and forcing the rest to rush too. 'No trap, the food is good.'

The good cell was always particular about niceties, even before eating a victim. 'Hi there,' it smiled. 'What kind of cells are you?'

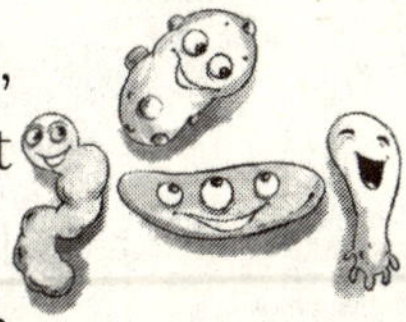

'We are the *Coli* cells,' said a group of panic-stricken tiny cells all lined together neatly in a circle. 'The *E. coli* cells.'

'Wow!' said the good cell cheerfully. 'You're the famous ones! The ones the researchers always used. Just like they are using us now, I suppose. Oh, I forgot to introduce myself – I mean, ourselves – we are the *Myxococcus xanthus* cells and we specialize in—'

Before it could finish the sentence, the *E.coli* cells started howling in pain and dissolving right in front of them.

'Hey, what did you guys do that for?' said the good cell, a little indignantly. 'I was just introducing myself and you send out your digestive juices! Is that any way to treat new friends?'

'Oh, of course not,' said the sarcastic cell. 'But it seems absolutely okay to eat your prey after you've become friends with them, is it?'

'Oh, stop squabbling, you two,' scolded the lazy cell. 'Wasting all your energy in discussing useless stuff.'

'Well, at least we got food,' the big cell gave a burp.

Suddenly they felt a huge shudder – almost like a big earthquake.

'Hey, what's THAT?' said the irritable cell. 'I hate this nonsense in the lab. They treat us worse than animals!'

'These humans think too much of themselves,' said the sarcastic one. 'They keep forgetting they've evolved from *us*.'

'Not only have they forgotten that, but also all the good qualities they had as single cells, or as a colony. All they do is fight with one another. And now they have to study us to re-learn the good things again!' The rest of them gazed in wonder at this outburst from the lazy cell, which was usually was too lazy to say more than a few words at a time.

The cells were no longer on a resting surface. The 'shudder' they had felt had drawn them up into a glass pipette, and they found themselves moving around freely in liquid. Then, just as suddenly, a force pushed them out of the pipette – *whoosh*!

Plop! They found themselves in a new field, along with other bacterial groups of their own kind. It looked like one of the researchers had picked them up along with many other cells and put them under the microscope for observation.

'This is a trick,' muttered the serious one darkly.

'What makes you think it's a trick?' asked the good cell. 'I don't think the humans are all that bad.'

'Look at the large number of us here. And see! There isn't a single bit of food here. We will starve!'

This was true. All around, they could only find barren stretches. No food at all.

They glided around for a long time, searching for food. But then they realized that all the other swarms were doing the same and were unsuccessful. And they realized their bodies were slowly turning circular, as they were becoming starved and undernourished.

'We will all die,' remarked the good cell sadly. 'I wish we didn't have to.'

'You won't have to,' came a new voice. All the cells in the swarm turned around. Two tough-looking rod-shaped cells stood before them.

'Just join the gang and clump together with the rest,' said one of them. 'We are just collecting everyone in one place.'

'Yeah, you will just stay asleep and inactive for a time inside this big group,' said the other tough-looking cell. 'And we are scout cells. We will cover all of you on the outer side and protect you like soldiers, look for food and wake you up when it's time.'

Thankfully, the group of bacteria huddled together along with the larger groups and went to sleep, while the scout cells stood guard.

A keen eye watched all this through a microscope. The eye belonged to Jose, a researcher. 'Hey, guys, look at this, they're forming a fruiting body!'

The rest of the lab continued with their work, while one or two raised their heads in curiosity.

More heads turned when Aaliyeh entered the room. 'Who's coming with me to the party now?' she announced breezily.

'Me! – Me too!' A bunch of interns and research assistants happily joined Aaliyeh and went out. The rest moped and sulked.

'They go off to enjoy themselves and we do the work,' said one.

'I say, what do we tell the professor when he comes in?' said another.

So when the professor walked in an hour later, he punished the entire lab – some for going out to party, and the rest, for letting them go. Jose too had to abandon his experiment to bear his part of the punishment – which was cleaning out the cages of the guinea pigs. The *Myxococcus bacteria* had a few hours of peace in their petri dish, not being prodded and starved by turns.

The scout cells, who observed the goings-on, laughed to themselves. 'Silly humans,' they said, giggling. 'If they'd worked as a team like us, they might have finished their work and had a party too!'

How do *the Myxococcus* bacteria manage to work as a team?

Myxococcus xanthus is a rod-shaped species of bacteria found in the soil, which preys on other bacteria. Though each bacterial cell is a separate unit or living organism on its own, several of these bacterial cells come together to form a group, as a response to different situations in their environment.

M. xanthus is 'saprophytic', which means that it absorbs nutrition from dissolved organic matter present around the cell. It secretes digestive enzymes that dissolve what it considers food (which includes other bacteria), so that it can then consume it!

Under normal conditions with abundant food, it exists as a predatory, single-species biofilm (layer of bacterial cells) called a swarm. A swarm of *M. xanthus* contains millions of cells that communicate among themselves in no particular pattern. But through a process called 'stigmergy', these bacteria communicate with each other 'indirectly' by giving biochemical 'signals', like slime trails, that pass on a message. This later builds up as more complex behavioural patterns among them.

For example, the tendency for one cell to glide only when in direct contact with another results in the colony forming swarms called 'wolf-packs' that may be up to several inches wide. This becomes an advantage to the members of the swarm, as it increases the concentration of extracellular digestive enzymes secreted by the cells, thus allowing it to feed like a predator.

Likewise, during stressful conditions, the bacteria undergo a process in which about 100,000 individual cells come together as a clump, to form a structure called the 'fruiting body' over the course of several hours. On the interior of the fruiting body, the rod-shaped cells turn into spherical, thick-walled spores that can survive starvation. Scout cells on the periphery guard the inner cells while also searching for prey.

14

EARTHWORMS ON STRIKE

'I won't wear that dress! ' said the little princess, turning her nose up high in the air.

'But, Princess, this is a beautiful dress,' said her lady-in-waiting. 'Besides, it is made of the purest silk, and the most expensive one in the kingdom.'

'I don't care,' said the princess unfeelingly. 'It has a smudge on it, and now the entire dress is spoilt. I can't wear it.' The 'smudge' was just a speck, tinier than the head of a pin.

'But, Princess, that is not a smudge.' said the lady-in-waiting, trying to appease her. 'That is a natural mark that appears when cloth is woven. And it's too tiny to be seen at all.'

'I want everything to be perfect and beautiful!' declared the princess. 'Throw this dress out and tell the dressmakers to make me another one exactly like this but without the mark.'

The lady-in-waiting hurried to inform the king of Princess Surya's new tantrum. On her way, she wondered if the selfish princess would one day bring about the doom of their rich and happy kingdom.

Surya was the princess of a beautiful and bountiful kingdom in the north, bordering the sea. The people in the kingdom were mainly farmers and the rest were artisans or tradesmen, while some were scholars. Every citizen was content and suffered no want. Nature had been especially kind to their land, blessing it with fertile soil and regular monsoons. Everyone was happy, especially as the land was ruled by a just king assisted by his wise minister.

But the king had a weakness – his only daughter, Princess Surya. He loved her dearly and pandered to every wish of hers. And now – as always – when the lady-in-waiting reached him with news of Surya's latest demands, he smiled indulgently and ordered that a new dress be made for Surya. 'However, to make up for the trouble,' he added, 'pay the dressmakers double their usual fee.' He felt that that was enough to make up for his daughter's behaviour.

The wise minister heard all this and was worried. He knew that the princess would soon be a young woman, and she would then have to take on some of the responsibilities of ruling the kingdom. If she continued her petty, intolerant behaviour, the people would suffer! He tried advising the king several times about this, but in vain.

'She's only a kid,' the king would say, 'She'll learn!' However, when exactly Surya would 'learn' was unclear, as she carried on the same way as before.

***

One day, Surya and her friends, along with some royal attendants, set out for a picnic in the gardens surrounding the palace, and the fields beyond. After playing on the swings for a while, they sat down to rest on the grass while the food was laid out. Surya was looking around her, when her eyes fell on something brownish pink and long, wriggling on the ground.

She went closer to have a look, and she found there wasn't just one but several of those strange creatures making holes in the ground and dragging themselves around in the soil. They were, in fact, earthworms.

However, Surya had never seen an earthworm before, so she cried out, 'What are these ungainly things here in the soil? They don't have hands or feet! '

'They are earthworms, Your Highness,' replied an attendant. 'They are usually found in the soil.'

'Yuck!' exclaimed Surya. 'How slimy and strange they look! These things don't even have eyes. Such revolting things should not be allowed in my beautiful kingdom at all!'

'Your Highness, please don't say so!' said the horrified attendant. 'These earthworms are the reason for our kingdom's prosperity. They help the farmers by digging deep into the soil, thus making the soil airy and moist, which helps the farmer till the land better. Our fruits, vegetables and grains are all of the best quality because these earthworms make the soil rich with their castings!'

'I don't care what they do,' announced Surya haughtily. 'They're too plain to be here. I henceforth banish all earthworms from the kingdom!'

Another attendant interrupted and said, 'Your Highness, you are still a princess. Only the king—'

Before she could complete her sentence, all the earthworms disappeared deep into the ground. They stopped burrowing and creating tunnels in the soil,

and refused to eat the garden and kitchen waste. Without their castings, the soil lost its fertility, and waste began to pile up. Surprisingly, the entire environment seemed to be siding with the earthworms, as there was no rain. No matter how much the farmers tried to irrigate their land, neither water nor air could circulate through the soil.

The hard-working creatures seemed to be on strike!

The news reached the king, who realized that this was a grave situation. He tried convincing Surya to apologize, but she refused. Despite the wise minister's repeated entreaties, the earthworms stayed underground. Very soon, the ground became hard and difficult to till. Many crop plants started dying, and the rest looked unhealthy and hardly gave any produce. To add to the woe, summer came upon the land and the intense heat killed whatever was left of all crops. Before long, the granary was empty and there was no food in the royal kitchen.

'I am hungry!' wailed Surya. 'Give me something to eat, please!'

'Nobody in the land has anything to eat, thanks to you, Surya,' said the king sadly. 'It is time you realize that every creature has been made a certain way to fulfil a special role in Nature. They may not seem flawless to us, but they are perfect in their own way. If only you hadn't offended the earthworms—'

Surya now understood what her father meant. She ran outside to the fields and called out to the earthworms, apologizing for her mistake. It wasn't long before the earthworms came up and called off their strike. And the kingdom went back to being prosperous again, with a wiser princess to rule it!

How important are earthworms?

Very!

Earthworms are invertebrates (without a backbone) and are called 'Annelids ' because of the little rings found on their body (*anellus* means 'tiny ring' in Latin). These worms have bodies that are segmented – and this gives the ring-like appearance. Earthworms create tunnels in the soil by burrowing, thus allowing water and air to reach the deeper parts of the soil. Earthworms eat the soil along with the dead and decaying matter present in it, like dead leaves. This matter is digested and excreted by the worms, which becomes 'humus' or manure for the plants. These excreta are called 'castings'.

There is a common myth that if an earthworm is cut into two, both parts become two separate earthworms. But this is false. Only the part with the head of the earthworm survives, and it can reproduce only if it is cut behind the eighteenth segment.

15

WAYS OF THE WILD WEST

The sun was setting in Oregon, North America, spreading a pinkish glow above the horizon. The twitter of birds as they made their way home to their nests filled the air. In the dark green fields of wild plants and grasses that were slowly folding up their flower petals and rolling up their leaves for the night, stood a few defiant little herbs – the wild tobacco plants called the 'coyote tobacco'.

Instead of preparing for a good night's sleep, they seemed to be preparing for a midnight party. They all had their leaves up and welcoming; their pretty white buds seemed all ready to flower. Only one little herb seemed a little unsure of herself. Her first small bunch of buds was ready to bloom that night, and the cold breeze that rocked her made her feel even more nervous.

'You'll be all right, kid,' a sudden voice behind her startled her. It was one of the biggest tobacco plants in the field, loaded with bunches and bunches of white buds waiting to blossom any second. Little Toe, as she was called, nodded in gratitude. 'Thank you, Auntie,' she said.

'Ah, you can thank me later,' said the bigger plant. 'We coyote tobaccos are tough ones, and we become strong because of all the challenges we face. There's a lot to come that you'll thank me for!'

Little Toe looked up in alarm. She had thought that not being eaten by the cattle that roamed the fields was enough of an achievement. The toxic, bitter taste of coyote tobacco plants discouraged most herbivores from even taking a bite of them! And yet, here was someone warning her of greater perils to come.

'Nothing to worry about,' said the 'Auntie' herb. 'I'll be here to guide you! But right now, pay attention to your first bunch of flowers – they're blooming!'

Little Toe was in for a beautiful sight. As darkness descended on the countryside, all the white buds of the tobacco plants started blooming, in perfect synchrony. The tiny white flowers now dotted the dark landscape like stars in the faint light of the rising moon.

'And, now, get ready to welcome your first visitors,' said Auntie to Little Toe.

'Visitors?' asked Little Toe, puzzled. 'But why should I have any? I don't know anyone.'

Auntie gave her an exasperated look. 'Don't you need any pollen to make seeds? Don't you want your own pollen to be taken away to other flowers? Can you do it yourself?'

'No, I can't,' said Little Toe, a little sheepishly. She had forgotten about making seeds that would give rise to more plants of their own kind.

'The problem is that these very helpers might turn troublemakers for us,' said Auntie in a worried tone.

But before Little Toe could ask how, the plants could hear a buzzing in the air. It was the sound made by the flapping wings of a host of sphinx moths, flying towards them.

'Here they come,' muttered Auntie, and every plant, every flower was taken over by one moth or the other. Little Toe had her own little flower cluster attracting two of them, and she stared in awe as they drank nectar and flew around covered in pollen. But the sphinx moths didn't seem to be leaving. Instead of just going away after visiting the flowers, a sphinx moth landed on one of Little Toe's green, fleshy leaves, and laid a few eggs!

At first, Little Toe felt all flattered. A mother had chosen her, to nurse her batch of eggs! New sphinx moths were going to be born in her shelter!

She voiced these opinions to Auntie, who gave an exclamation of utter disbelief. 'Are you crazy, kid?' she asked. 'Do you want to die even before you grow up properly? Once the eggs hatch, the hornworm caterpillars that come out will feed on every bit of those juicy leaves you possess now!'

Little Toe was shocked. 'There's nothing you can do though,' muttered Auntie darkly. 'Wait till they hatch.'

A few days passed, and finally one day, out came innocent-looking green caterpillars. But unlike the bigger animals that hated the taste of the tobacco plants, the caterpillars seemed to love them! A bite here and a bite there, and poor Little Toe was in tears. But Auntie consoled her.

'Don't bother,' she said. 'They're inviting their own doom, those little creepers.'

With each bite by the caterpillars, Little Toe's panic increased. She could feel the changes in her body – not just physically, but also chemically. It looked like the wounds on her leaves had caused her to let out some strange chemicals, and their smell hung in the air.

But Auntie wasn't in the least perturbed. 'Now watch the fun,' said Auntie, giggling.

To Little Toe's surprise, there came to the field a whole new group of insects – the big-eyed bugs.

'They're our friends, you know,' whispered Auntie to her. 'They can smell the chemical signals we let out of our leaf wounds. They'll take care of our problem.' And just like she said, the bugs started feeding on the hornworm caterpillars and eggs, without causing any harm to the tobacco plants.

'Oh look, the Cotesia wasps are coming too!' cried Auntie gleefully. Little Toe now saw wasps coming to their rescue. Instead of eating up the caterpillars, they laid their eggs on the caterpillar's back!

'Those wasp babies are going to eat the caterpillars inside out,' said Auntie. 'Now we will be rid of this nuisance!'

Thankfully for Little Toe, her tormentors were destroyed soon enough. But it wasn't that easy for Auntie herself, who had many, many leaves, and many, many caterpillars still living on her.

'Oh, Auntie!' cried Little Toe. 'What are you going to do?'

'Do?' Auntie laughed. 'Why, I'm going to give them a gift!'

'What gift?' demanded Little Toe.

'A nice, smelly gift,' said Auntie. 'See these hairs I have? Well, you have them too – they contain nectar – which these caterpillars like very much. It's so tasty, they can't resist it. But there's just one problem. They start smelling too, and become really juicy and tasty themselves – and sure to attract their enemies here!'

And just like she predicted, the caterpillars had the nectar and started smelling like a very inviting dish. So it was no wonder when a few more bugs and other enemies turned up to finish off the remaining caterpillars. Only very few caterpillars finally managed to survive and become sphinx moths!

***

That year, Little Toe made her first seeds. She was awfully happy, and she had grown bigger, with more flower clusters blooming on her! She was no longer the shy, ignorant little herb she had once been.

'I managed it, Auntie,' she said one day. 'All thanks to you! But I still worry about one thing: What do we do when there are just too many of these caterpillars and we can't handle them anymore? They are a necessary evil, after all, and we can't do without them either!'

The bigger plant looked thoughtful. 'You know, kid,' she said, slowly. 'Things don't remain the same always. This is what we have done for generations to survive.

But sometimes, old ways just don't work anymore – you need to change. It will have to be a drastic change, no doubt, but I've heard of many coyote tobaccos who did it, and survived. Instead of blooming at night, they started blooming in the day. And the sphinx moths don't fly in the daytime, see? So they're safe! They no longer attract the moths with their flower scent. They got other insects to take away their pollen instead.'

Little Toe pondered over this for a moment. 'That's a great idea, Auntie,' she said. 'If things get too bad, I'll start blooming in the day! But tell me, what if, one day, all the sphinx moths learn to fly in the daytime too?'

Do plants and insects keep learning new behaviours to adjust with changing conditions?

Yes, they do! *Nicotiana attenuata*, or the coyote tobacco, is a species of wild tobacco found in the western regions of North America and in northern Mexico. An annual herb, which is hardly noticeable, apart from its property of producing nicotine that is stored in its leaves, this plant has a long list of defences to protect itself from its predators. The presence of nicotine itself renders it poisonous, and the bitter taste prevents herbivores from grazing on these plants. The nicotine in this species is three times higher than in normal tobacco plants.

Two species of insects – *Manduca quinquemaculata* and *Manduca sexta* – commonly known as California sphinx moths, are not just its main pollinators but also its main predators. Their larvae, known as hornworms or Goliath worms, are immune to the high levels of nicotine, and feed voraciously on the leaves of the plant. However, when the plant is attacked, it releases certain volatile compounds from its wounds into the air, called 'Green Leaf Volatiles' (GLVs), which act as warning signals not just to other plants but also to the predators of this caterpillar, signalling their presence. Big-eyed bugs (*Geocoris species*) descend on the plants, and feed on the hornworm caterpillars and eggs.

The parasitic wasp, Cotesia, also lays its eggs on these caterpillars, and the resulting larvae feed on the caterpillars internally, thus killing them. If the GLVs don't work well enough, the caterpillars consume the nectar present in the plant hair and let out further signals that attract their predators. And, as a last resort, some of these plants start blooming in the daytime so as not to attract the sphinx moths at all!

16

THE CRANE'S CONTACT LENSES

'So...shall we be friends?' Cookie asked the hesitant stranger in front of her. Cookie was an adorable little duckling and all the ducks in her pond felt she was the cutest little thing they had ever seen. Cookie wasn't proud, but she was quite pleased with all the admiration she got. She had soft yellow feathers, innocent blue eyes and a tiny, soft, pink bill. Besides, she was sweet-tempered too – and so, was sweetly asking the new foreign kid in her pond if they could be friends.

'Uh –yes, I think so,' said the foreign baby bird a little awkwardly. 'But we are so different. I am a whooping crane and you're a duck.'

That was quite true. The baby whooping crane, whose name was Bubbles, looked nothing like Cookie. She was a dirty brown all over, with a pointed beak that seemed just a wee bit too large for her face. Her gait was awkward, and she didn't really have proper feathers yet. Her family was visiting the marshy meadows on the other side of the hill, and she had wandered over to the duck pond.

'But both you and I have blue eyes,' said Cookie happily. 'That's something we have in common!'

'Same pinch,' cried Bubbles, laughing, and the two were soon having fun together. After a while, Bubbles heard the cries of other cranes. 'I think I have to leave now,' she said. 'But I'll come again soon!' she promised, and she left.

***

Three months passed. Cookie had grown, but no longer looked as cute as she did when she was a baby. She was neither yellow nor white and was at an awkward stage. Her parents told her it was a passing phase. And that was when Bubbles came to visit her again.

Bubbles was still brown but had grown quite tall. Both chatted for some time and played a bit, and that was when Cookie noticed something different about Bubbles. Her eyes were no longer blue. They looked greenish grey! Cookie was puzzled. Before she could ask Bubbles anything about this, it was time for her to go, and she flew away. After Bubbles left, Cookie pondered over the colour of her eye. How could the crane's eyes turn greenish grey when they had been blue in the beginning?

***

Three more months passed by, and Cookie was a fully grown duck now. She now had a beautiful white coat of feathers and a yellow beak, but the same blue eyes. One day, as she was looking at her reflection in the water and preening, she heard a flap of wings behind her.

'Surprise!' cried a voice, and Cookie turned around to find a really, really tall bird, the tallest she had ever seen, with a pure white coat of feathers, a red crown and black wing tips. It was striking – glamorous, even.

It took a moment for Cookie to recognize her visitor. 'Bubbles!' she cried and hugged the whooping crane. Both were thrilled to see each other and had a wonderful time together. In the midst of all the fun, Cookie keenly observed Bubbles's eyes. She was shocked to find that the crane's eyes were now no longer blue or greenish grey. They were, instead, *golden*.

Cookie didn't know how to ask Bubbles about it. All throughout the conversation, she could think of nothing but Bubbles' amazing transformation, while she herself seemed as ordinary as the rest of her flock. She was especially envious of Bubbles' changing eye colour and wondered how she had managed it.

One day, she could no longer control her curiosity and spoke to her friend, the frog, about it. He thought deeply for a while and said, 'I've heard of something that the humans use for changing their eye colour – they call it contact lenses. Do you think Bubbles has got hold of those?'

Cookie wondered if that was true. 'Then I can change my eye colour too and look at least a little bit as stylish as Bubbles?' said Cookie eagerly.

'Maybe you can,' replied the frog, 'but how are you going to find such a thing?' This made Cookie morose again.

'You just want to look different from your flock, don't you? Forget your pride and ask Bubbles herself when she comes next time.' Saying this, the frog hopped off.

Cookie thought of this suggestion. She realized she could never look entirely like Bubbles. After all, she was just a duck – she could never grow as tall as a whooping crane! But it didn't seem a bad idea to try out the contact lenses. So the next time Bubbles came to visit her, Cookie braced herself to ask her about it.

At first, she hemmed and hawed, and then finally asked, 'Bubbles, could you...erm...please...tell me... where you get your contact lenses?'

Bubbles gave Cookie a blank look. 'What contact lenses?' she asked.

'Well, the ones you wear, to change your eye colour from blue to grey to gold,' said Cookie.

Bubbles looked even more puzzled. And then, all of a sudden, she burst out laughing!

'Don't laugh!' said Cookie angrily. 'Tell me if you can, and it's fine if you can't,' she said, pouting.

'Oh, Cookie,' said Bubbles still roaring with laughter, 'who told you that I wear contact lenses? That's how we whooping cranes are! We are born with blue eyes, which change to a greenish grey after a few months. When we are full-grown adults, our eyes turn gold in colour!'

Cookie was dumbstruck at first. And then she started laughing too. 'How stupid I am!' she said, good-natured and sweet-tempered once again, and the two friends laughed about it for a long time.

Does the eye colour of whooping cranes really change?

Yes, it does!

Whooping cranes are the tallest of all birds in North America, and also the rarest cranes in the world. It's name comes from the 'whooping' call it makes with its mate. They frequent marshes, lagoons and shallow lakes. They feed on fishes, frogs, shellfish and small insects.

Whooping cranes are an endangered species, due to indiscriminate shooting of the birds and destruction of their habitat in the prairies, where more and more land is being used for farming. Conversion of wetlands or marshes to dry land by artificial means and severe droughts due to climate change have also caused the population of whooping cranes to decline. Efforts are on by researchers and environmentalists to restore their population.

Eye colour in whooping cranes, like in several other bird species, changes during the course of their lifetime, and why it changes is still a mystery! At birth, their eyes are blue, which change to aquamarine or a grey/greenish hue as they grow older, and after six months, when they become adults, their eyes turn golden or bright yellow in colour. In some birds, like the red-tailed hawk, it changes from yellow to red–brown; in the American crow, from blue or blue–grey to brown; in the sharp-skinned hawk, from bright yellow to red, and so on.

The reasons behind this could lie in their genes, or the way these traits were selected as 'better' during evolution, or simply due to the presence (or absence) of certain pigments, oil droplets, lipids, blood vessels and so on in the iris. It could just be a marker of their maturity, which shows that they've turned into adults, helping them find potential mates; or it could be an adaptation to suit their plumage colour to increase camouflage; or a result of bird hormones, where the colour is linked to their reproductive cycle.

17

NATURE'S GOLDEN CALCULATIONS

Thirteen-year-old Amit Varma looked at the completed diagram with satisfaction. He hadn't thought he had the talent for it, and he wondered why he hadn't given much attention to his pencil-wielding skills before.

He held the paper up against the light and admired his handiwork. The skeleton seemed to be looking at him with its hollow eyes and giving him a toothy grin.

'Bhaiyya, are you done?' asked nine-year-old Akash, his younger brother, eagerly.

'Just a few touches here and there,' said Amit pompously. 'Then I'll give it to you.'

Amit had never been one to pay much attention to drawings or diagrams of any sort. His science record books were often incomplete, with remarks in red from teachers. His drawings looked more like doodles of wiggly squiggles and haphazard lines.

Not that it mattered to him. He pooh-poohed those who studiously worked on their records and drawings, and turned his nose up at those who got awarded the 'gold star' for their work.

His attempt at drawing the skeleton was only spurred by the unwavering adulation he got from Akash, and he felt he couldn't ignore his request of helping him with his homework.

Akash looked on as Amit added some shading here and there to the bones of the skeleton's limbs.

'There you go,' he said at last. 'You're sure to get a gold star!' Amit proudly waved the diagram of the human skeleton, spindly and eerie in all its glory.

'Thanks, Bhaiyya!' squealed Akash in joy and hurried to paste it in his notebook.

***

It was mayhem the next evening at the Varma household. Akash had come back in tears, his trust in his older brother completely eroded.

'The teacher said it looks nothing like a skeleton,' sobbed Akash, 'and my classmates who saw it were sniggering too.'

'I'm sure it's not all that bad, sweetie,' said his mother, wiping his tears. 'But why did you make Amit do your homework in the first place?'

'Because I didn't have the page with that particular diagram in my science textbook,' said Akash, sniffling.

'It's been torn out... I asked Bhaiyya because I was running out of time.'

Amit turned red. The textbook Akash had was *his* old one, a hand-me-down, and Amit *had* referred to his own diagram (a very basic one) from his old record book. He had just tried to improve on it using his own imagination.

'Well, I really did do my best,' said Amit defensively. 'And I was only trying to help.'

'That's not how you help,' said his mother hotly. 'Akash should be doing his homework himself! How will he learn otherwise?'

Just then, their father came in, and all three of them turned to him with their complaints and explanations. Their father asked them to tell him everything from the beginning. Then, he asked to see the famous diagram that was the cause of all this misery.

One look at it and he burst out laughing. 'Ha-ha-ha,' he hooted uncontrollably. 'Hee-hee-hee, ho-ho!'

'*Hmmph*,' said their mother, pouting. 'Instead of helping them, you are making a joke of the whole thing.'

'Well,' said their father, wiping away tears of mirth, 'just see for yourself...'

Amit's skeleton was like no human skeleton that ever existed in the history of the earth. It had abnormally long arms and legs, while the skull was puny in comparison. Its knees and elbows stuck out at odd angles. Overall, it *did* seem comical.

'*Hmmph*,' said his mother again. 'I keep telling you to practise, Amit—'

'I guess we should look beyond books to draw better,' said their father. 'Come on, boys! Time for a walk. And get your notebooks and pencils too!'

Both boys followed their father outside.

***

They came to the old lily pond in the middle of the building courtyard.

'Do you boys see those snails crawling along the walls there?' asked their father, pointing to a few snails. 'Try drawing them in your notebooks now.'

Amit immediately drew an oval shape for the body of the snail, and a few large concentric circles on top (if they could be called that!) to indicate its shell. Akash took a little while more, and managed a very shaky-looking misshapen shell, without any discernible body.

The father looked at their work. 'Now let's go closer and have a proper look at them.'

Amit and Akash peered closely. They looked more or less the same!

But then they saw that each snail's shell was a beautifully shaped circular shell, whose spiral became larger and larger with each coil. 'See the difference?' said their father.

Then their father took them to the sunflower fields in the nearby valley. 'Remember how you both drew the sunflowers in the birthday card you gave me? You just scattered some dots for the seeds, with petals all pointing upwards for florets! That's fine for a rough sketch, but Nature is so much more organized in its beauty. Look closely now!'

The boys found a set spiral pattern in the florets of the sunflower. Even the seeds at the centre had two spirals, one clockwise and the other counterclockwise.

'Now look at the trees,' said their father. 'Do you find the branches growing too close together or too far apart?'

'No,' said Amit slowly, 'they all seem to split at specific intervals, and it seems to depend on the size of the branch too—'

'Bravo!' said their father, smiling. 'You're getting an idea of how proportion works in Nature.'

'What's proportion?' asked Akash.

'In simple words, it's a ratio. And in this case, it's called the "golden ratio", said their father. 'Nature has its own way of ensuring the most pleasing symmetry in its living creatures, which are all built by the golden ratio calculation – at least, that's what a lot of people have thought in the past. Your limbs are an example of this golden ratio, simply called 'phi,' which has a value of 1.618. That means, if you measure your entire arm, and then divide it by the distance from your elbow to the tip of your fingers, you will get this value. The same applies to your legs.'

'What? Really?!' Both the boys were astounded.

'Yes,' their father continued, 'this is why Amit's skeleton looked funny – he did not draw the limbs or head proportionate to the body.'

'So is that what we saw in the snails, flowers and branches too?' asked Akash.

'Yes,' said their father, 'they naturally follow by a pattern that follows the 'Fibonacci sequence' – a series of numbers where each number is the sum of the preceding two numbers. Divide each number in the sequence by its previous number, and you get the golden ratio!'

Realization had dawned on Amit and Akash. 'So we should just make use of this principle for our diagrams!' said Amit happily.

'Yes, skeletons will thank you forever!' said their father jokingly and all three of them had a good laugh.

Does Nature really follow a golden rule?

Yes, it does!

The famous Fibonacci sequence is a favourite idea of mathematicians, artists, designers and scientists alike. Also known as the golden ratio, its presence is felt everywhere in Nature. The golden ratio is a number that's equal to approximately 1.618. This number is now often known as 'phi' and is expressed in writing using the symbol for the letter phi – which looks like Φ – from the Greek alphabet.

The Fibonacci sequence goes by this sequence of numbers: 1, 1, 2, 3, 5, 8, 13, 21, ... The first interesting thing about this sequence is that each successive number in this sequence is obtained by adding the two previous numbers together. The second interesting aspect is that, when dividing each number in the Fibonacci sequence with the previous number, the result obtained is the golden ratio.

The golden ratio is found abundantly in Nature. Apart from being the basis of symmetry in human bodies, it is also the basis for the number of petals in a flower, the seeds produced in spiral patterns (as in sunflowers), seed pods on a pinecone, tree branches, spiral shells of the snails, the spirals of galaxies and hurricanes, and even our own faces.

18

D.B. TO THE RESCUE

It was another sunny day at the Bovine Farm. Brown, white and black cattle often roamed the fields, munching grass, but today, the farm looked deserted. And it was not just the grounds that were empty. For miles around, there was no animal in sight.

Right then, a flock of pigeons flying overhead, which had just crossed over to the area surrounding the farm, stopped mid-air. All of them felt an overpowering stench. 'Yuck!' they cried, all together, 'This place smells strongly of dung!' And they immediately changed their course and flew away in another direction.

Betty Cow, who had seen the pigeons' reaction from her window, shook her head resignedly. It was a terrible problem, and it looked like there was no solution to it.

Betty Cow and the other cattle, who had spent a long time wandering from place to place, had finally found a peaceful home in the middle of a green valley.

There was plenty of fresh grass to eat and no wild animals nearby to attack them. Plus, the sheep farm was nearby too, and they came over off and on.

In the beginning, everything had been fine. There had only been a few cattle, and they managed very well with what they had. But soon, their number increased, so much so that they had a new problem. Food didn't matter; it was always in plenty. But the problem was 'dung'.

Once the number of cattle had gone up, the amount of dung they all deposited had gone up drastically too. The dung had piled up so much that the entire farm smelled badly. Earlier, only the cattle were aware of the problem. But as the mountain of dung increased in size, so did the smell. And the cattle didn't know what to do. The sheep, who had been regular visitors earlier to the farm, were nosy neighbours and soon found out that there was something wrong with the cattle farm.

'Why does it stink so much?' they asked.

Betty and the other cattle told them, 'Oh, that's a strong smell carried here by the wind.'

But of course, the sheep were never convinced and tried all their tricks to find out the reason. Each time they came to visit, they found an excuse to wander around the farm, and looked here and there to find the source of the stench, all the while holding their noses. And one day, they found the huge pile of dung! And what a ruckus they created!

'Untidy animals, the whole lot of you,' grumbled the sheep, in a half-mocking, half-disgusted tone. 'You cattle don't know how to clean up!'

The cattle were quite sad, because of course, they were not like that. If they could have roamed from place to place like they had done earlier, all that dung wouldn't have piled up.

***

The cows stayed inside their homes day and night, hardly venturing out, partly out of fear of being laughed at by other animals, and partly because they couldn't stand the smell of the dung themselves!

Betty was just going to close the window after listening to the pigeons' conversation when she heard a tiny voice whispering.

'Shhhh...here,' said the voice.

Betty strained to find out where the voice was coming from. Finally, she realized it was a small insect, a beetle, standing on the windowsill.

'I bring you good news,' said the beetle. 'You've got an enormous amount of dung that needs clearing? Fear not!'

Betty looked at the beetle questioningly.

It's D.B. to the rescue!' cried the beetle in a voice as loud as he could manage and tried to swirl around with the air of a superhero.

Betty was quite astonished by the antics of the tiny insect in front of her.

'Who's D.B?' she asked.

The beetle seemed highly offended at her ignorance.

'Who? Who? Why, I am D.B.!' he cried, agitatedly. 'And the whole world knows it,' he added, and sat down, hands folded and a mutinous look on his face, as if that established his fame and position.

'So what can you do?' Betty asked him, a little apprehensively.

'Like I said, I am D.B., the Dung Beetle,' said the insect, 'and my job is to dispose of the dung at different places. I caught the smell of your delicious dung—' He stopped. 'Sorry,' he added hastily, and continued, 'well, tasty for us, anyway – and I thought you might need some help to clear it off. You just have to say the word, and I will be back with my team to do away with it! Can I start off immediately, please?' He gave Betty a pleading look.

Betty was quite unsure of what to say.

'But you're so small!' she said. 'How can you clear such a huge pile of dung?'

'I sure can, along with my team,' said D.B. earnestly. 'Trust me!'

Betty couldn't answer immediately. She had to ask the other cattle too.

'Well then, just let the starling know when you make up your mind!' said the beetle. 'She knows where to find us.' He went scuttling away.

Betty was just going to inform her friends when there appeared the sheep from the other farm.

'We thought we should help you,' said the sheep, 'so we thought of telling you about the dung beetles in our farm who clear away the poop...er...dung. So let us know if you need them.' Saying so, the sheep ambled away, their noses screwed up to avoid the stink.

Betty consulted the other cattle. They all decided that recommended candidates were always better, and called the dung beetles of the sheep first. But when they came, all of them abandoned the task within a few minutes. One of them turned to the cattle and said, 'I'm sorry we can't clean this. This is cattle dung! We are used to cleaning up the remains of...er...just sheep.'

Another said, 'The sheep didn't tell us it would be cattle dung we had to clean up! We had told them earlier that we couldn't clear anything other than the excreta of the sheep! '

The cattle were aghast. How could the sheep be so mean to them?

'I guess we will have to call D.B. to the rescue then,' sighed Betty.

No sooner had she called D.B. than he came charging in with his retinue of dung beetle followers. All the dung beetles set to work. One group, called the 'rollers', rolled the dung into little balls and rolled them away with their hind legs into burrows. Another group,

called the tunnellers, buried the dung balls in the ground. Yet another group, called the dwellers, neither rolled nor burrowed. They just lived in the dung! The cattle watched in wonder as the army of dung beetles cleared away their pile of dung in a few hours. It was quite remarkable!

At the end of it, Betty and the other cattle could not thank the dung beetles enough.

'I'm sorry I underestimated you,' apologized Betty.

'Well, now you know – just call me anytime you need me,' said D.B. with a smile. 'D.B. to the rescue!' he cried, and he vanished. And since then, Bovine Farm has never stunk.

What are dung beetles?

Dung beetles are insects that eat dung.

They are found on every continent except Antarctica. Though they may not eat only dung all the time, they lay their eggs in the dung and their larvae feed on it, getting the required nutrients from the excreta. Though humans may find this icky, these beetles play a great role in ensuring that the excreta of the many large animals living on this earth is removed, thus contributing to a cleaner environment.

There are three types of dung beetles: (1) the rollers, which pack the dung into circular balls and roll it with their hind legs till they reach their burrows in the ground, (2) the tunnellers, who bury their dung balls in the ground, and (3) the dwellers, who live in the dung. There are several species of dung beetles, and each species eats only a specific type of dung and no other!

About 200 years ago, when the human settlers in Australia set up farms to rear horses, cattle and sheep, they faced a huge problem with the disposal of dung, because the dung beetles of Australia were used to eating only the excreta of kangaroos! The settlers had to bring in exotic dung beetles from their homeland, which could feed on the excreta of horses and cattle, to clear up the waste on their farms.

19

AN OILY TRICK

'Nana, you're so clever – wish I could be like you,' said Pitchy the pelican to his best friend, Nana. It was break time at Bird School. Several different baby birds attended it to learn different things like finding prey, putting up a good defence against enemies, building strong nests – in short, everything that a bird needed to know.

'Nana does well in every class,' said Vicky the vulture, another classmate of Nana's, while heaving a big sigh. 'The only class I manage to get decent grades in is the "Scare your Enemy" class.'

'You get decent grades there because your enemy is half-dead anyway,' giggled a parrot. 'How much more can you frighten them?'

Vicky grimaced.

'She gets the highest grades in the "Finding food" class, though,' said the pigeon.

'That's because she only eats the fruits of the oil palm – things that don't run away from her when she goes after them,' said the vulture spitefully, quite annoyed that everyone was talking so highly of Nana.

'Yes, but remember she gets them at night, not in broad daylight,' said the pigeon.

'She has sharper eyes than any of us – she can see equally well during the day and at night,' said Pitchy. 'She is the only nocturnal fruit-eating bird in the world!'

'Then what about bats?' said the vulture grumpily. 'They eat fruits too, and they do so at night.'

'Bats are not birds, dumbo,' said Pitchy. 'They are mammals. Now you know why you are at the bottom of the class.'

Vicky got up to leave. He was very annoyed. He hated Nana, the wonderful bird who seemed to possess every good quality in the world.

'Oh, and by the way, Nana can find her way at night just like bats do – using sounds and their echoes to find obstacles in her path!' called out the cuckoo to the vulture as a parting shot.

Nana blushed with pleasure at the praise showered on her by her classmates. Nana was an oilbird, a unique bird which lived on the island of Trinidad in the Caribbean Sea. Nana was a naturally brilliant student, blessed with multiple skills that set her above the rest of the class. But she was very modest and simple, and innocently brushed aside the words of her friends.

'Don't glorify me so much,' she said shyly. 'All of us have different qualities and abilities. None of us is greater than the rest.'

The other birds nodded in appreciation. They were proud to have a talented, humble and large-hearted bird like Nana among them. Laughing and talking, the entire class went out to play.

***

Meanwhile, Vicky was brooding over the discussion that had taken place in class. He was upset that he was the weakest student in the class. The teachers scolded him every day, asking him to learn from Nana. And now his classmates too were making fun of him. If a bird like Nana hadn't been in the class, there would be no model student for anyone to look up to and he wouldn't be ridiculed any more.

The more he thought about it, the angrier he became. He began to think of Nana as the root cause of all his problems. He wondered what he could do to worry Nana in return. He couldn't do anything to Nana openly; he would get into worse trouble. What else could he do then? Maybe, worry her so much that she couldn't be her clever, bright self? How could he do it? He thought about it for a long time. And, slowly, an idea shaped up in his mind, and he decided to put it into action.

After the break, when everyone was back in class, Vicky went and sat beside Nana. It was not his usual place, and Pitchy frowned when he found him sitting next to *his* best friend. But he said nothing and sat at the desk behind Nana.

While the class was in progress, Vicky turned to Nana. 'You eat those oil palm fruits, don't you?' he asked. 'Aren't they full of oil?'

Nana eagerly turned to him. 'Yes, that's what I eat,' she said joyfully. 'They are really tasty, and my mother says that our bodies are rich in oil too!'

Vicky put on a grave look. 'Just as I thought,' he said in a low voice.

Nana was puzzled. 'Why, what's wrong, Vicky? Oil fruits are nice. In fact, I eat more of them than anyone else at home. Maybe you should try eating them too one day.'

Vicky gave her a frightened glance. 'Oh no, thank you,' he said hoarsely, 'I cannot take such a risk. It is simply terrible.'

Nana asked anxiously, 'Why, Vicky, what's so terrible about oil palm fruits?'

Vicky gave Nana a pitiful glance. 'I'm only worried about you,' he whispered in a sad tone.

'Worried about me?' demanded Nana. 'Why, what's wrong with me?'.

'I have heard many vultures talking about it,' said Vicky slowly. 'In recent times, many corpses have been found with high oil content in them. I heard my parents saying that those were people who died due to a condition called 'high cholesterol'. The cholesterol in their body increases due to their food habits and they die of something called a heart attack.' He looked at her seriously.

'So? What does that have to do with me?' asked Nana.

'Since you eat so much of oil – I mean, these oil palm fruits – your cholesterol levels must be very high by now,' said the cunning vulture. 'I don't think you have much time left to live!' He nodded in sympathy before moving away to his usual seat in class.

Nana was shocked. She thought of all the fruits she had eaten and wished she hadn't had so many. She

turned pale, thinking that she was going to die soon. She sat through all the classes in a haze. When the teachers asked her questions, she either kept silent or gave the wrong answers. It was a very bad day for poor Nana.

Vicky, who had been watching Nana the whole time, rubbed his hands in glee. He had succeeded in tormenting Nana enough to destroy her mental peace.

***

Pitchy noticed Nana's strange behaviour but didn't know the reason behind it. The usually cheerful Nana was now gloomy and inattentive. That evening, he went home with her. Nana's mother had set out an evening snack made of oil palm fruits for Nana. However, she didn't touch it.

'Why aren't you eating, Nana?' asked her mother.

Nana burst out crying. 'I can't eat this,' she said, 'I'll die!'

Nana's mother was surprised, and so was Pitchy. 'Who told you such things?' asked Pitchy.

'Vicky did,' said Nana, between sobs, and the whole story came out. 'Our bodies are full of oil because of these fruits, Mummy. And just like humans who eat lots of oily stuff, we will die too!'

Nana's mother laughed. 'We have the ability to digest fats and use them for our nutrition,' she explained.

'That's how Nature has built us. We won't die because of the excess oil.'

'And tomorrow I'll teach that dreadful vulture a good lesson that he'll never forget!' said Pitchy, and all of them had a good laugh.

What are oilbirds?

Oilbirds are the only nocturnal, flying, frugivorous (fruit-eating) birds. They are found in the northern parts of South America, including Trinidad, an island in the Caribbean Sea. Though they feed mainly on the fruits of the oil palm and tropical laurels, they also eat a variety of other fruits. Unlike other birds, oilbirds are active during the night. During the day, they rest on ledges in caves to digest their food.

Chicks are exclusively fed on a diet of fruit pulp, making them fatter and heavier than the adult birds. These birds absorb 80 per cent of the lipids (fats) in their diet, leading to a build-up of fat in their legs. Indigenous Americans captured oilbird chicks and melted the fat to extract a pure form of oil, which was used to light torches.

While oilbirds have eyes with the highest light-gathering capacity compared to any other bird, they also have the unique ability to navigate by 'echolocation' in the dark – just like bats – where they emit high frequency sounds and judge the obstacles in their path by the echoes reflected back to them. The only other bird that uses echolocation is the cave swiftlet found in the forest caves of South Asia.

20

A JAIL FOR SNAILS

'And of course I followed his track of slime and found him in no time!' cackled Clyde, and all the other snails burst into laughter. 'The clown thought I wouldn't find him if he hid under that big leaf!'

'And then you made lunch of him whole – shell and all?' inquired Pesco curiously.

'Nah! I sucked him out of his shell,' said Clyde. 'Took a bit longer, of course, but then it's a more aesthetic way of eating, I should say.'

'Like humans using chopsticks or forks to eat their food instead of grabbing it with their bare hands,' said Miguel, the snail who was considered 'the brain' of the group, but also the gentlest ('More like a coward,' was Clyde's opinion).

'My lunch yesterday was a garden snail,' boasted Pesco. 'It was quite big! But it left an awful taste in my mouth.'

'Yuck! That variety gives me stomach ache,' said Clyde.

Clyde, Pesco and Miguel were rosy wolfsnails or 'cannibal' snails, which survived by eating other snails. They found their prey by following the trails of slime left by other snails, and either swallowed them whole or sucked them out of their shells. Moving at a speed of 8 millimetres per second, these snails were faster than all other snails, thus letting them hunt other snails and feast on them. The three were comparing notes on who had eaten what that day.

'I am bored of these snails here,' moaned Pesco. 'How I wish we had the chance to try some new snail cuisine!'

'Ha, fat chance!' sneered Clyde. 'We'd have to travel so far and so long that we'd probably die before we came across a new variety to hunt!'

Pesco looked at Miguel for support. 'He's right, *amigo*,' said Miguel gloomily. 'Only a miracle can grant you your wish!'

***

As luck would have it, the next day, the three snails found themselves captured and packaged away in cages on a ship. Miguel, who could understand human language, carefully listened to the conversations of the humans on board, and came back with the news.

'You lucky scoundrel, you!' Miguel gave a smack to Pesco. 'All you had to do was wish for it, and here we are, on our way to Hawaii!'

'What? For real?' Clyde was shocked. 'You must be joking, right? Whoever listens to this loser here and decides to give him a treat?'

'Wow! I never thought my wish would come true so quickly,' remarked Pesco.

'Yeah! We're going to try out new snail cuisines in Hawaii!' cried Miguel, and the three snails did a small victory dance right there (which took about half an hour, given their pace).

'Are you sure, Miguel?' Clyde asked after a while. 'You're sure the humans aren't planning to eat us?'

'Positive,' replied Miguel confidently. 'Apparently, there's a population of snails called the giant African snails in Hawaii that's causing the humans some trouble. They want us to get rid of them.'

'Did you say "giant"?' asked Pesco, his mouth already watering at the thought.

'Giant means juicy too,' said Clyde dreamily. 'Never thought we would get such an opportunity. And of course we mustn't disappoint them; I already have an appetite, and it shouldn't be hard to finish off the snails they want to get rid of.'

***

When they reached Hawaii, the rosy wolfsnails were let off in the fields to fend for themselves.

'The giant snails must be found here,' said Miguel wisely. 'That's why they left us here. I heard that they were pests, and ate the crops and other useful plants.'

'Well, no wonder they want us to get rid of them,' said Clyde.

Pesco was already scouting for slime trails. 'Here, you guys, come here!' he called. 'Have a look at this huge slime trail.' Sure enough, on the wet ground, they found a milky white trail of slime, thick and copious. 'Well, just this once, guys, let's hunt him together,' pleaded Pesco. 'We don't know anything about these new snails, and it would be best if we kept together.'

Clyde and Miguel looked at each other. 'I think we should do as Pesco says...' began Miguel, but stopped as soon as he saw Clyde's scowl.

'Please, Clyde,' begged Pesco. 'Look, you're our leader and the bravest among us. I know I found the trail, but you can have him if you like. Just this once. After this, we will split up to find our own food.'

Finally, Clyde gave in. 'Alright,' he said, 'let's follow this one and see how it turns out.'

The three snails diligently followed the slime trail, and soon came across a large snail, much bigger than them, feeding on the stalk of a plant. It saw them but paid them no attention.

'This... This snail is big...far too huge,' stammered Pesco as soon as he saw it. 'How is any of us supposed to eat one this size?'

'It doesn't even seem scared of us,' muttered Miguel. 'We are right behind it and all it does is ignore us

instead of running away. Is it because it thinks it's too big to be eaten by us?'

'I don't see why I can't eat it,' said Clyde haughtily.

Pesco and Miguel gave him dubious looks. 'But I don't want to,' Clyde said hastily, taking a step back. 'It somehow...doesn't look inviting. And food should look good.'

'Tell me once again why the humans wanted to get rid of this?' asked Pesco.

'Well, look at that ugly thing,' retorted Clyde. 'Who would want it in their garden?'

Miguel began, 'Well, I heard them say it's because these giant African snails eat up useful crops and also spread a disease called meningitis in humans when consumed... .'

'What?' Clyde and Pesco were both dumbstruck with horror.

'Meningitis?' Clyde repeated hoarsely.

'When...when consumed?' Pesco was almost in tears.

'You want us to eat that...that thing?' Clyde was shaking Miguel furiously. 'No way we are going to eat a disease-carrying snail! You are the one who said it's going to be a feast here and all that nonsense. If I starve, I am going to eat you!'

Miguel desperately looked around for escape. 'Hey, look! Look at those smaller snails there! What are those?'

The tiny snails with colourful shells were bunched up on a tree trunk. Pesco stealthily went closer and listened to their chatter. He came back with the information.

'They are Kahuli tree snails, native to Hawaii,' he said.

'They seem good enough to eat,' said Clyde thoughtfully.

'And just the right size,' added Pesco.

'Aww, they look so cute, I don't feel like eating them,' said Miguel in a baby voice.

Pesco and Clyde glared at him. 'Do you want to eat those giants then?' Clyde growled.

'No, no, that's not what I meant,' said Miguel, hastily.

So, soon all the rosy wolfsnails who had been brought down to Hawaii started eating up the Kahuli tree snails, and years passed. The rosy wolfsnails multiplied in number, while there were fewer and fewer Kahuli tree snails left...until there were hardly any.

***

One day, Miguel came back with urgent news for his friends. 'The humans are angry,' he panted. 'They are upset we ate up all the Kahuli tree snails and not the giant African ones. They say that the Kahulis used to eat the harmful fungus on the trees and shrubs, and now their forests and fields are being destroyed because of the fungus.'

'Pah!' spat Clyde. 'It's our wish what we eat and what we won't. So what are they going to do about it?'

'They have built a jail for snails,' said Miguel fearfully. 'They are already on their way, collecting up snails, I heard. I am scared we'll be put in jail too, for eating the Kahulis.'

They could hear men walking through the forest, talking among themselves. 'Here they come! Hide!' said Pesco.

But of course, the humans were much faster than the snails. A gloved hand came close to where they were.

'This is the end,' thought Clyde. But instead of snatching them, the gloved hand caught some Kahuli snails that were sitting on a nearby tree. The men walked on, collecting the Kahuli snails in their baskets as they went by.

'You mean, we're the culprits, yet the Kahulis go to jail?' cried out Pesco gleefully.

'Either way, *amigo*, we're going to starve,' pointed out Miguel gloomily. 'So much for international cuisine.'

Can snails be cannibals?

Some species of snails are!

Kahuli tree snails (Genus *Achatinella*) are tiny molluscs that are native to Hawaii, and are found only on the island of O'ahu. They are very small, with colourful, elongated shells, which are less than an inch in length. They only eat fungus that grows on the leaves of trees and shrubs.

The giant African land snail that was accidentally introduced in Hawaii turned out to be an invasive species that voraciously fed on crops and plants, and is considered an agricultural pest. These giant snails were cooked and eaten by humans; when not cooked properly, they caused meningitis in people.

In order to combat the menace of the giant African snails, the rosy wolfsnails or cannibal snails (*Euglandina rosea*), which were native to Central America and specialized snail-eaters, were introduced in Hawaii. Unfortunately, they preferred to prey on the smaller Kahuli tree snails found in abundance on the island, leading to the extinction of at least eight Achatinella species, and several others, overall comprising 60 per cent of the original 750 species of the snail population.

This disrupted the entire ecosystem at Hawaii as the Kahuli tree snails feed exclusively on fungi and decaying matter. The trees and plants have become weak due to severe fungal infection. All of the remaining Kahuli species are now being protected in a 'jail-like' enclosure where they cannot be hunted by the cannibal snails.

21

A LEAF OUT OF NATURE'S BOOK

'Hey, Chester – not that way, boy, come here!' George called to his dog, as he jogged up the path carved out in the public park. Several joggers passed him as he slowed down, waiting for Chester to come to him. However, there was no sign of his golden retriever.

'Chester...' he groaned. He retraced his steps to find his dog. 'Gone after that rabbit,' he muttered to himself. He looked around, trying to spot his dog. But Chester was nowhere to be seen. Other joggers and morning walkers looked at him curiously as he started parting bushes and undergrowth that lined the paths, to look for his dog.

'Chester, are you there... oops! I'm sorry, ma'am, I didn't mean to upset your umbrella –

'Chester, where are – I hope I didn't step on your foot, sir, my apologies—'

At last, searching and stumbling, he found Chester stuck in a bramble bush, whining and trying to wrench himself free.

'Oh, you silly dog,' George scolded Chester gently and slowly wrested him free. The thorns of the bramble bush cut into his hands, but he didn't mind. Poor Chester was injured too, and all that George could do was cut short his morning exercise and take him to a vet. On the way, George tried to clean him. Chester's fur was full of burrs, which stuck completely to it and stubbornly refused to come off.

The vet tut-tutted, shaking his head in exasperation. 'All those burrs need to come off, or I can't clean his wounds,' he said, and George and the vet together managed to pick all the burrs from Chester's wound.

'Why, Mr George, you have them all on your coat too,' commented the vet, as he finished treating Chester. That was when George noticed how the burrs had stuck on to his clothing too! How did they manage it? However, there was no time to ponder over it, for Chester was now back to normal and licking his face enthusiastically.

***

The next day, George was back at work as usual at the engineering company where he worked. He had a lot of tasks to complete and forgot all about the incident.

After long and hectic months at the office, he finally managed to steal some time for a holiday. He set off with Chester by car to the Swiss Alps, all ready to spend at least a week in that serene beauty.

When they reached the woods close to the Alps, George parked his car and started off on his hike with Chester, taking only his backpack with him.

'The Swiss Alps, old champ – what better place for a hike, huh?' George asked cheerfully, as Chester bounded faithfully beside him. Both dog and master thoroughly enjoyed their walk through the woods, with Chester often chasing some mountain hares or marmots. George let him go on his adventures, and

waited patiently for him to come back and join him. Away from work and responsibilities, George had all the time in the world.

Towards noon, he decided to stop for lunch. As he sat down on a rock and opened his pack of sandwiches, he realized there was something bothering him. Chester, who had obediently sat down in front of his master, waiting for a bite, couldn't stop scratching himself.

'It's those burrs again,' said George thoughtfully, trying to calm Chester down. Chester's fur was once again full of tiny burrs that stuck on. George found the same burrs stuck on his clothing too.

'Looks like these seeds naturally cling on to whatever they can, so that they have a better chance of going and growing far from the parent plant,' pondered George. He quickly collected the burrs into a small glass bottle and got up with a firm resolve.

'Chester, our holiday's cancelled,' he announced, while Chester looked at him questioningly and wagged his tail. It was only when George took him all the way back and bundled him into the car that he realized the full meaning of George's words. He whined in protest, while George hurried home.

His tail between his legs and his head drooping, Chester followed an excited George back inside the house. Whatever had taken over his master, thought little Chester. George hadn't even offered him a sandwich. And the smell had been so delicious!

George, meanwhile, headed straight for his small laboratory. He put the burrs under a microscope and peered keenly at them. He found that the burrs had hundreds of 'hook-like' structures! He slowly tried placing the burrs on cloth, his hair, and Chester's fur too. But each time, they stuck. All they needed were loops into which they could attach their hooks! How wonderful it would be if he could bind two different materials together, using the same trick that the seeds used to get around!

***

From then on, George used all his time to master a technique to make synthetic materials that could act just like the burrs. All he had to do was take two sheets of a material, one of which would have hooks and the other would have loops.

But alas! It was easier said than done. When he presented his idea to other engineers, they laughed at him.

'How is that possible?' asked some.

'What's the point?' asked others.

But, much to Chester's chagrin, his master kept at it, sparing hardly any time for his beloved pet.

The work on the 'hooks' and the 'loops' went on for eight long years. George tried out his idea first with cotton, but unfortunately, cotton did not last long. He decided to experiment with synthetic fibres instead.

He finally decided that nylon was the best option as a fabric to replicate Nature's trick.

At long last, his idea was ready in a practical form. It took him an additional two years to mechanize the mass production of the product he had invented. He named it 'Velcro,' and had to wait for five years to get a patent. But when he did get it, the idea of using Velcro gradually caught on in a number of ways and in various businesses. Shoes started to be fastened with Velcro, clothes too, and even astronauts used it to fasten their unwieldy and heavy spacesuits! Velcro had become a great success.

George was finally at peace. He thought about how Chester had (even if accidentally) played a great role in showing him the possibility of such an invention. He climbed up the steps two at a time that night to bed, and paused to give an extra pat to Chester, his faithful dog through the years.

'Hey, Chester,' he whispered, 'we did it.'

Was the invention of Velcro inspired by Nature?

Yes, it was!

Fabric hook-and-loop fasteners, named 'Velcro' after the company that produces them, were invented by Swiss engineer George de Mestral in 1941. The idea for his invention came to him when he went on a hike with his dog (an Irish pointer named Milka) and found the burrs (seeds that have hooks or teeth) of the burdock plant (*Arctium* species) clinging to his clothes and his dog's fur.

The burr has several tiny hooks on its surface, which fasten tightly to any surface that has loops. It is a mechanism of seed dispersal employed by the plant, called epizoochory, where the seeds are dispersed by attaching to the fur/outer surface of animals.

However, this is just one instance of biomimetics, which is a branch of bioengineering.

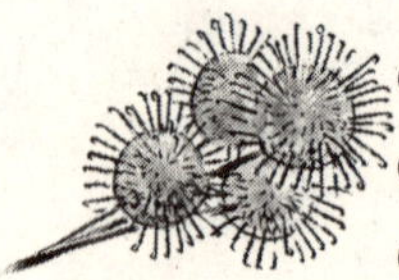

Biomimetics draws inspiration from Nature to design advanced technological products. Principles from engineering, chemistry and biology are applied to the creation of new materials, synthetic systems or machines that mimic natural, biological processes. Neural networks in computers are based on the neuron networks in the brain and their working; aeroplanes were built by the Wright brothers after observing birds and their flight; and dirt and water-repelling paints have been modelled after lotus leaves, which have microscopic, hydrophobic (water-repelling) bumps with a waxy coating to repel dirt and water. Biomimetics has many uses, especially in medicine and surgery, such as gecko-inspired surgical glue and a needle inspired from a parasitic wasp.

Recently, scientists at the Indian Institute of Technology – Guwahati have developed an oil-repulsive coating for wood, glass and metal surfaces that will keep them oil-free under water – the technology was inspired by fish scales, which remain oil-free even if the water is contaminated with oil, thus protecting the fish.

22

THE STRANGE NEW NEIGHBOUR

'I was going by that scrub forest when I just got a glimpse of him – or her – I don't know which,' said the kangaroo to her neighbour and friend, the parrot. 'I couldn't even make out what kind of animal it was.'

It was late afternoon, and chit-chat time for the kangaroo and parrot. The parrot especially enjoyed these sessions, because she flew around the whole forest telling other animals what she had seen or heard from someone else. And each time she told the story, she added her own juicy titbits to it, making it sound more and more bizarre, until the final version was something completely different from the first. However, things had been dull for many months and the parrot hadn't been able to get her claws on anything sensational for a long time. So this bit of news about a new neighbour in their locality made her feathers quiver in excitement.

'Well, if you saw the creature, you could have made out something about it,' said the parrot. 'At least whether it was an animal, a bird or a reptile?'

'Actually, I just saw its tail,' said the kangaroo. 'And I was quite puzzled, because...' The kangaroo trailed off.

'Because?' the parrot leaned in eagerly.

'Because the tail belongs to an animal that simply cannot be found on our continent!' ended the kangaroo.

'Why, what do you mean? How can that be possible? You must have been mistaken. What kind of tail was it? Thin, long, thick, striped, furry, bushy?'

'None of these, I tell you,' whispered the kangaroo. 'It was...flat!'

'Flat? What kind of animal has a flat tail?' asked the parrot, quite astonished.

'That's exactly what I mean,' said the kangaroo, her eyes wide. 'The tail I saw belongs to an animal called the beaver. And beavers are not found in Australia!'

'Do you think the beaver has migrated here?' asked the parrot.

'Who knows – maybe it's had enough with the humans in the northern hemisphere,' the kangaroo sighed heavily.

'I'm going to have a look at this creature myself,' said the parrot determinedly. 'Since I can fly, I'll get a good bird's-eye view. Meet me by the pond in an hour's time!'

***

The parrot flew off, wondering how a beaver could have got to their land by swimming across the oceans. She hovered high over the forest, squinting around. She could see the kangaroos jumping around with their babies in their pouches; the red foxes lazing around in the sun; the squirrels nibbling on nuts; and the fish frolicking in ponds. But there wasn't a sign of this strange creature that the kangaroo had told her about.

She was just about to descend when, very near the pond, she spotted an animal she had never seen before in the area. It was half hidden by the bushes and she could only see its body. Then it slid off again into the undergrowth and the parrot couldn't see anything more.

She flew to the pond hurriedly, where the kangaroo was waiting for her.

'Did you find it? What is it?' The kangaroo sounded eager and impatient.

The parrot gave her a pitying look. 'I really don't know what's gone wrong with your eyes, my dear,' she told the kangaroo. 'You must be getting old if you can't make out the difference between a beaver and an otter!'

'What? Impossible!' The kangaroo was flabbergasted. 'No otter has a flat tail like the one I saw.'

'Well, I'm sure you have made a mistake about the tail – I just saw its body,' said the parrot, 'and that is just like an otter's, right down to the fur. So now I know that you're really growing old. I thought we had a new neighbour, but instead I have an old friend with poor eyesight.'

'Oh, you're just making up stories like you do every time,' cried the kangaroo, working herself up into a frenzy. 'I should never have made friends with you!'

The parrot was no less shocked at the kangaroo's outburst. 'I've told stories, yes, but never about you, my friend,' she said in a bitter voice. 'How can you be so mean?'

'Ha! So you admit that you tell stories!' cried the kangaroo angrily. 'How does it matter whom you spoke about till now? I'm sure you'll talk about me next to the whole forest!'

'Yes, I will,' said the parrot defiantly. 'I'll say you're old and more. I'll tell everyone that your fur is worn out, but you coat it with mud and make it smooth and youthful. I'll tell everyone that you lost all your teeth and you're wearing dentures. I'll tell—'

'Oh, stop it, stop it, both of you!' screamed a voice. It was the fish who lived in the pond. 'Stop fighting. I don't think either of you is right anyway.' He came closer to the bank. 'I've seen the new neighbour too, when he waded through this pond, and I know what creature it is,' said the fish proudly.

'What is it?' cried the kangaroo and the parrot in unison.

'Why, it's a duck!' said the fish triumphantly. 'I could see it as soon as I saw its bill and its webbed feet that it used underwater here to paddle along.'

The parrot and the kangaroo stared blankly at the fish as he went on in his confident voice, 'And believe me, what a large bill it was! Flat and rounded like a duck's. And its feet? Beautiful, webbed feet, all four of them gracefully moving in the water like synchronized dancers—'

At this point, the parrot stopped him. 'Pray, Mr Fish,' she said, 'what kind of duck has four feet?'

Mr Fish stopped speaking. He swallowed once or twice, trying to figure out if his eyes had deceived him. At last, he said, 'Well, I'm still sure it must be a duck.'

'It jolly well isn't,' intercepted the kangaroo. 'It was a beaver!'

'No, an otter,' cried the parrot, not one to give in.

'No, a duck, I tell you, it was a duck!' cried the fish.

The three started squabbling again, so loudly that half the forest gathered to watch them. Nobody dared to stop them, until a voice suddenly called out, 'Are you all talking about me?'

The kangaroo, the parrot and the fish turned to find their new neighbour emerging from the crowd. They stared open-mouthed and unabashed at the stranger in their midst. It had an oblong body, with a big flat beak that was shaped like a duck's bill, and webbed feet, just as the fish had said; a flat tail like the kangaroo had observed; and dark brown fur covering its rounded body like the parrot had insisted.

'Why, it's a platypus!' cried someone in the crowd.

'A platypus?' repeated the kangaroo and the parrot, quite stumped by what they saw. The fish couldn't stop opening and closing its mouth repeatedly.

The platypus didn't seem to mind all the attention it was getting. 'Yes, I'm a platypus. I have an otter's body, a duck's bill and webbed feet, and a beaver's tail. I am quite blessed to be a combination of many things apart from being a mammal that lays eggs! All of you were right, but only partly. If you had seen me entirely, you might have guessed what I am. After all, platypuses are common here in Australia!'

Are platypuses really a mix of so many features?

Yes, they are!

The platypus is one of Nature's wonders – a unique combination of characteristics that seem to have been borrowed from different animals!

In fact, when the platypus was first discovered in Australia and sent to London for scientific study, scientists believed that someone was trying to fool them by sending them a mammal's body with a duck's bill sewn on to it! Even when they realized that such a creature did exist, it took some time for the scientists to accept that it was a mammal and not a bird or a reptile.

Platypuses (*Ornithorhyncus anatinus*) are one of the five living 'monotremes' left in the world today. Monotremes are primitive mammals that lay large yolky eggs. Platypuses are about 15-20 inches long, and the webbed feet and tail help them to swim in water. These webbed feet are retractable, and on land, they reveal their nails, which help them run.

They don't have teeth, so they scoop up insects, larvae, shellfish and worms from the ground along with some gravel and mud, and it is this gravel which helps them 'chew' their food, by grinding it down. Their sensitive bill helps them to find food.

The male platypus also has a poisonous spur on its hind foot, which it uses to claim its territory during the mating period and also to warn off any predators such as crocodiles, Tasmanian devils and raptors.

Analysis of the platypus' genes gave some interesting information: they carry mammalian, reptilian and bird genes! Platypuses are the farthest relatives to mammals. While it was earlier considered the missing link between mammals and reptiles, its genes show that its egg-laying traits evolved from birds, while it retained mammalian characteristics as well.

Although sharing a common ancestor (Therapsids – mammal-like reptiles) with the marsupials and mammals, monotremes broke off from other mammals about 166 million years ago through evolution. Their most unique features, however, evolved on their own, as an adaptation to their surroundings.

23

LAND OF THE BLOOMING STONES

'Please get some water from the stream, Phenny,' said Annika, who was trying to light a fire in the kitchen.

'Why should I get the water? You get it,' said Phenny, who was lazing around on the straw mat outside their mud hut, chewing a piece of grass. 'You were the one who used to get water when Mama was here.'

'I would have got it myself, Phenny,' said Annika patiently to her younger sister. 'But I have a lot of work to do here, and it would be a great help if you could just fetch the water. Be a dear and do it for me.'

'I won't,' Phenny said defiantly. 'I shouldn't even be living here with you in this dirty hut. Remember what that wise old man said? He said I would become an heiress to a great fortune one day. I'm going to be rich! And wealthy heiresses don't do menial jobs like fetching water from the stream.' She pouted stubbornly.

Annika sighed. Annika and Phenny were two sisters who lived in a small village in Namibia. Ever since a mysterious old man had predicted a bright future for Phenny, she refused to do the simplest of jobs around the house. Their mother, who also believed the old man's words, had set out one day in search of her long-lost brother, who she said was a rich merchant in a far-away land and would probably make Phenny the heiress she deserved to be.

Annika set out to the stream herself, hoping her mother would be back soon. It was already a month since their mother had left home, and Annika was worried. She was hardly bothered by Phenny's royal tantrums because her mother occupied her thoughts all the time. As she reached the stream, she heard someone coughing loudly in the nearby bushes.

Surprised, she peeped through the shrubs. It was the same old man who had come to their hut. She hurriedly collected some water in the pot and rushed to help him. The man stopped coughing as he drank the water Annika gave him.

'God bless you, my child,' he said in a hoarse voice. 'I did not expect anyone to come to my help.'

'That's alright, Grandpa,' said Annika, smiling.

The old man looked into Annika's eyes. 'But you need help, my child,' he said gently.

'Oh no, Grandpa,' said Annika cheerfully, 'what help could I possibly need? I am fine.'

'Maybe you don't need it yourself,' said the old man solemnly, 'but your mother does. She needs you.'

Annika was shocked. What could have happened to her mother?

'Why do you say so, Grandpa?' she asked, full of worry. 'What's wrong with Mama?'

'Nothing will go wrong if you go to her soon,' he said gravely.

'Oh, but we don't know where she's gone!' wailed poor Annika 'How will we find her? We don't know where our uncle lives'.

'Just follow my instructions and you will find her,' said the old man. 'Cross this stream and go through the forest. You will find a path that leads you to the Namibian desert. Follow the clouds during the day and cross the desert until you come to a valley surrounded by high rocks. That is the Land of the Blooming Stones. When the stones on the ground bring forth flowers, you will find your mother too.'

Annika looked in the direction that the old man was pointing to. She shivered at the thought of travelling that far, crossing forests and deserts. And blooming stones! She had never heard of such a thing!

'But, Grandpa, how can stones bloom?' she began. 'They aren't plants—' Annika turned to look at the old man again, but he had disappeared!

'Grandpa? Grandpa, where are you?' Annika called out several times and searched all around for him, but he was nowhere to be found. Annika decided she could not waste any more time. Their mother needed them and they had to hurry!

She rushed back home and shook awake Phenny, who was dozing outside the hut.

'Get ready to come with me now,' cried Annika, packing all that she could think of. 'We have a long journey ahead of us.'

'Uhh...What journey?' asked Phenny, yawning. 'Where to? Why?'

'Mama needs us,' said Annika. 'We need to find her!'

Without waiting to explain any more, Annika dragged Phenny along with her. Annika followed the directions of the old man, and along with Phenny, managed to cross the stream and the forest without much difficulty. However, with Phenny whining all along the way, the journey was no easy task. Annika felt it was easier to handle the wild animals in the forest than deal with Phenny's complaints.

***

By the time they reached the desert, a month had already gone by. The sun shone down more harshly than ever on the two girls, and the dry winds of the desert made the trek miserable. Both girls were tired and Phenny was annoyed with her sister for making her life miserable. She tried her best to talk Annika out of it.

'Let's go back,' Phenny pleaded. 'I think this is all nonsense. Do you think Mama would come all this way, through forests and deserts, to reach her brother's home? How can you blindly trust the words of a stranger?'

'Well, you didn't mind believing the old man when he told you that you'd become an heiress one day, did you?' replied Annika impatiently.

Phenny scowled but kept quiet after that. All she wanted to do was get back home. She made up her mind to escape from her sister when she got the chance.

Annika, however, was determined to reach her mother at all costs. At last, they reached the valley that the old man had spoken of – the Land of the Blooming Stones. The ground was covered in stones and pebbles of all colours, shapes and sizes. But there wasn't a single flower to be seen.

'Well?' questioned Phenny, her hands on her hips. 'Where are the stones that bloom? And where is Mama?'

Annika sank to the ground, exhausted. She wondered what she had done wrong. Wasn't this the place they were supposed to come to? Why weren't the stones blooming like he had said?

'I told you this was a wild goose chase,' said Phenny harshly. 'Who has ever heard of stones that bloom? Stones are not plants to bring forth flowers. Stones are not even living things. How could you fall for such rubbish? We have come so far away from home just because of your stubbornness.'

Annika was too upset to even reply. The food and water they had got from home was almost over. She stared blankly at the rocks and stones, hoping they would speak up and come to her rescue. But of course they didn't. The empty valley echoed with Phenny's words, and Annika closed her eyes tight. 'Let's wait for a few more days,' she pleaded with Phenny. 'They might bloom after all.'

The two sisters waited day and night, with Annika hoping for a miracle. Autumn passed and winter descended. It was terribly cold and the sisters huddled together for warmth. They'd finished their stock of food, and survived on nuts and berries that they found in the valley and by sparingly drinking the water from their very last bottle. But they still couldn't find any change in the stones.

One morning, when Annika woke up, she found Phenny missing. She realized that her sister had left. On her own now, Annika once again tried to find flowers among the stones. She could find nothing. She went to sleep crying that night, thinking she would die soon of cold, thirst and sadness.

That night, it rained. The next morning, when Annika woke up, to her pleasant surprise, she found that many of the pebbles were blooming with beautiful daisy-like flowers! The floor of the valley

was now covered in a lovely carpet of yellow and white blooms. With a cry of joy, Annika bent down and picked up one – only to realize it wasn't a pebble, but a plant that looked like one!

As she gazed in wonder, the first rays of sunlight fell on the wet rocks surrounding the valley and they moved aside, revealing a path to a large, beautiful villa. And Annika saw, to her great joy, her mother standing right at the door of the villa, waving at her! She rushed forward through the passage into her mother's arms, and the rocks closed over once again, concealing the Land of the Blooming Stones.

Are there really plants that look like stones?

Yes, there are!

They are called Lithops. These plants are made of just a root system and a pair of leaves that have evolved to hold as much water or moisture as possible so that the plant does not die during the hot summer months. To perform this function better, these leaves have lost their original form and have become more rounded, like a pebble, thus minimizing evaporation of water as much as possible. Found in Namibia and southern parts of Africa, these plants mimic the colour and appearance of the soil and stones around them, to avoid being eaten up by plant-eating animals, as bright colours would attract attention to them easily.

Most Lithops produce their flowers during autumn and early winter. They are daisy-like and yellow or white in colour. Also called 'Living Stones', they belong to the plant family Aizoaceae (say *ay-zo-ay-si-eye*).

24

PUSHING AWAY PLASTIC

Shiv's mother was already up and about at 5 a.m. Shiv could hear her banging down utensils on the stove and the countertop in the process of cooking for the family.

'Wake up,' his mother prodded him with a spoon.

Shiv groaned. 'It's too early, Ma,' he said.

'Your board exams are around the corner,' she chided him. 'Start studying!' She hurried back to the kitchen. Shiv dragged himself out of bed and sat down in the hall facing the kitchen.

Shiv's father, Vinod, sauntered in sleepily. 'What's the hurry, Ranjini?' he asked his wife, yawning.

"Have you forgotten?' she said, grimacing. 'My brother's coming today. Even though they're here only for half a day before catching their next flight, *I'm* the one who has to rush through work – make breakfast, pack your lunches, and then go to the railway station.' She vented her feelings on a potato as she chopped it into tiny pieces.

Vinod put on the most winning smile he could muster. Taking the knife from her hand, he started dicing the potatoes. 'I haven't forgotten, dear. It just slipped momentarily from my mind.'

Then he turned to Shiv. 'And you, young man, should be waking up at 4 every day to study. When I was your age, I would wake up at least two hours before the rooster crowed, read my lessons for the day and—'

'Alright, Dad, I know, I know,' said Shiv hurriedly, sensing an oncoming lecture. He rubbed the sleep from his eyes and muttered under his breath about his miserable life.

'This boy doesn't take anything seriously!' complained Ranjini. 'I don't know how he's going to fare in his exams—' She gave a small exclamation as she saw the state of the potatoes under Vinod's knife. 'What have you done to those potatoes?' she grumbled. 'It's better I do it myself. Now I have extra work to do.'

Shiv sniggered in a corner and his father threw a rolled-up newspaper at him. Shiv hurriedly poked his nose back into his textbook.

'Why don't you take the garbage out?' Ranjini asked her husband. 'Wait – let me give you these vegetable peels too.' Ranjini scooped up all the kitchen waste into a plastic bag and handed it to Vinod, who dutifully dumped it into the garbage bin, before gathering it all up in another old plastic bag to leave it outside for the pick-up van.

'Did you throw away those old shaving blades like I told you to?' called Ranjini from the kitchen again. 'And the broken glass frame?'

'Sure did,' answered Vinod.

Shiv, who'd been watching everything, felt uncomfortable when he remembered what he had learnt in class.

'Mom, you shouldn't be putting all the waste together like this,' began Shiv. 'Put dry waste, wet waste and medical waste in separate bags. And you should be using biodegradable plastic bags, not these thin ones you get from the local vendors—'

'Do you think I have the time to do all that?' grumbled Ranjini. 'Tell your father.'

Shiv called out, 'Dad, why don't we buy those biodegradable plastic bags? They'll be much more environment-friendly and—'

His father stopped him mid-sentence. 'We've been managing all these years like this – does it really make a difference?'

'Yes, Dad, it does...' Shiv said, 'to the poor creatures affected by plastic pollution!'

'At least we are packing up our garbage properly and getting it picked up!' his father said. 'Look at Savita-ji who dumps garbage in the empty plot – do we do such things? You're bothered about everything in this world except your studies.'

The doorbell rang in the middle of the reprimand. It seemed to be a delivery executive. Shiv hurriedly moved away. These were dangerous times, he thought. Any topic could be connected with his forthcoming board exams.

'Ranjini, coffee, please?' Vinod requested. 'I need to leave early for work today.'

Ranjini's trials seemed endless. 'Of course, you'd have to go earlier today, as it's *my* brother who's visiting,' she said drily, as she cut off a tiny corner of a milk packet 'Your lunch is ready. Don't forget to take it!'

Vinod looked at the packed lunch box on the table. It looked like the curry would surely drip into his bag and soil his office documents. He had always hated it when, during his schooldays, his mother would tie up his tiffin box in a square cloth napkin. The *sambar* and the *rasam* would seep through into his books – so embarrassing! *Thank God for plastic bags*, he thought.

'Ranjini, where are the plastic bags?' he said.

'They're here behind the kitchen door,' said Ranjini. 'But I'm running out of stock now.'

Sure enough, Ranjini had a huge plastic bag full of neatly folded plastic bags: extra-large, thick ones she got from the supermarket at the cost of 3 or 5 rupees each; thin and transparent blue and black ones she got from the local grocer; and smaller ones she forced out of the vegetable seller. She kept them all for future use, despite her son's arguments against plastic.

Plastic bags made her life easy, because they made good carry bags, garbage bags and gift covers.

'I'll get some extra plastic bags from the vendors,' said Vinod, as he waved bye.

'Ask for separate ones for each item!' called Ranjini from inside.

***

At long last, Ranjini saw Shiv off to school and finished her chores in time. At the railway station, she received her brother and his family warmly.

She listened intently to their news as she helped them check into a hotel, after which she took them on a tour of the city, then to the beach where she bought them ice cream and cool drinks (with plastic straws for the kids, of course) and, all in all, ensured they had a great time.

'Aunty, where do we throw these straws?' asked one of her nieces.

'Oh, just throw them in the gutter, dear.' The child promptly aimed the straw into the sea. The grown-ups laughed indulgently.

That evening, Ranjini passionately narrated the details of her brother's visit while Vinod fished out the several 'extra' plastic bags he had got from grocery and vegetable vendors.

Shiv eyed both of them warily. 'Whale dies in Thailand after consuming more than 80 plastic bags,' he read out loudly from the newspaper.

Vinod frowned. 'So what? That's far away in Thailand, not here...'

'Stop preaching against plastic, Shiv – you don't understand how convenient our life is because of it,' said Ranjini.

'At the cost of the lives of several creatures on land, and in the sea and air, Ma,' said Shiv. 'Birds, marine creatures, cattle and other animals eat plastic unknowingly, and it either kills or suffocates them. Microplastics affect the lungs and their ability to

produce offspring. And plastics also leach chemicals that are harmful to not just other creatures but for our health too! Yet you refuse to change.' Shiv went away in a huff.

Ranjini and Vinod stared after him.

'The boy seems really upset about this,' said Vinod. 'Shall we...?'

Ranjini made a sulky face. 'I can't change all of a sudden,' she said. 'Alright, let's buy the biodegradable plastic bags and make a start.'

What happens if we use plastic for everything?

The invention of plastic gave the world a material that is lightweight, flexible, moisture-resistant, strong, relatively inexpensive and, most importantly, long-lasting. In fact, it lasts so long that we cannot get rid of the used plastic on earth! Plastic is extremely slow to degrade, and most plastics we use are non-biodegradable (i.e., they do not break down naturally).

About 8 million tonnes of plastic waste are disposed of in the world's oceans every year, which is like throwing an entire truckload of plastic into the sea every minute, every day. More than half comes from Asia, where much of the world's plastic is produced, consumed and discarded. Marine waters are becoming garbage dumps for the world's plastic, forming 'garbage patches' the size of small countries. Sea creatures often mistake plastic for prey and end up eating it, or choking on it. Plastic litter on land damages soil and is often eaten by unsuspecting animals or birds, suffocating them or killing them by blocking the digestive tract.

Eighty per cent of the plastic in oceans comes from trash blown from the streets, garbage bins or landfills into rivers, sewers, or directly into the ocean. However, it also comprises microplastics (tiny fragments of plastic less than 5 mm in size) from products like toothpaste or synthetic fibres from clothes.

In India, 25,000 tonnes of plastic waste is generated every year, and only 60 per cent recycled. If we learn to use alternatives for plastic we can hope for cleaner rivers and oceans. Even a small gesture like not snipping off a corner of the milk packet can reduce plastic pollution by a great measure, as these small pieces cannot be recycled and often end up as waste in the soil or ocean. By doing our bit, we can ensure a better life ahead for future generations of both animals and humans.

25

THE HORNBILL WAITS FOR RAIN

It was June; a year in the 1980s. Dark clouds gathered above the green forest somewhere in south India, blocking out the glaring sun, ready to burst forth their showers after a long and tiring spell of summer. They sent out loud thrills of thunder, drumrolls summoning every being out of slumber. They sent their flashlight signals of lightning streaking across the darkened sky, hoping that it got the attention of the right creatures. The earthy scent called petrichor, which rose from the parched soil as the first water droplets descended, announced that more rain was imminent.

Then the clamour began. The frogs in the forest lake chorused *ribbit-ribbit* in joy. Elephants trumpeted, and the peacock shook out its glorious plume of feathers, ready to dance. The clouds rejoiced at the welcome.

Yet they waited for one particular friend of theirs. They'd heard that no one wanted rain as badly as the hornbill did. So they looked anxiously for the black bird with its large, yellow, curved beak, and the funny yellow cap. Soon enough, they saw it fly up to the highest branch of a tall rosewood tree, looking up expectantly at them.

'You've come!' they cried joyfully, as they let go of torrents of rain.

'Of course I have,' said the hornbill. 'How could I not, when my friends the rain clouds are doing a great job?'

'We love to bring joy to everyone!' said the clouds.

'And you do!' said the hornbill. 'Tell me, where are you going next?'

'Some of us are going on an exchange programme,' giggled one of the clouds. 'We plan to visit the USA and Canada and Europe—'

The hornbill looked very happy for his cloud friends. He wished them luck and flew away. By then, the clouds had finished their quota of rain and they asked the wind to take them to their next stop.

'That was a jolly good shower, wasn't it,' said one cloud on the way.

'Yes, it was. But, I say, did you see the hornbill drinking rainwater this time?' said another.

'No I didn't!' said a third cloud. 'I watched closely last time too, but he never drank any then either.'

'Then why do they say that the hornbill can't drink any water except by tilting its head backwards when it rains?' said the second cloud again.

'Does it really matter?' asked the first cloud. 'All I know is that the hornbill is our friend...so there!'

The other clouds agreed and continued on their way. It would take years for them to finish their tour and come back to their home in South Asia.

***

At first, everything seemed wonderful to the clouds. Instead of trees and mountains, they saw skyscrapers, industries, factories, flyovers, airplanes and train stations – all made with advanced and high-end technology. But when the clouds rained down over the countries and forests there, something didn't seem right.

The lovely petrichor was clouded by a more acidic stench, and the sulphur dioxide and nitrogen oxide gases emitted from the factories and power plants seeped into them. They couldn't understand it at all when people started covering themselves with protective clothing when it rained, instead of dancing and rejoicing; and when the forests started to decay instead of brimming with greenery. The fishes in the lakes were dying, and scientists worriedly pointed out buildings and bridges that seemed to be corroding.

***

'Acid rain,' the scientists announced on the news. 'The rain falling here is no longer pure water. It's contaminated with sulphuric acid and nitric acid. It is harmful for our ecosystem, and we must fight it!'

The clouds had been blissfully unaware of this, until one day they realized that the birds had stopped flying through them and, instead, avoided them as much as they could. When they asked the birds, they said, 'It's all over the news!'

The clouds were shocked and dejected. What were they to do? They had gone near the industries and factories, and the sulphur dioxide and nitrogen oxide from them had been in the air! The gases had mixed with their raindrops as the clouds let loose their showers. The rain had turned to acid for no fault of theirs!

The scientists and the heads of various countries had organized meetings all over the world to discuss how to stop the acid rain. But the clouds could see no hope.

'A bad name is a bad name,' said one cloud darkly. 'No amount of rain can wash it off.'

'Don't be silly,' said another cloud. 'Can't everyone make out it's not us, it's these gases from industries?'

'Bad news and gossip travel faster than the truth,' said a third cloud. 'Don't be surprised if our friends in Asia hear all this and desert us!'

This plunged the clouds into fresh sorrow, as it was time for them to go back. What would they all say? Would they greet them like before?

Unknown to them, the scientists and leaders of countries had already started work to minimize acid rain. They cut down emissions from factories and industries, and spread the word to ensure that the such pollutants were minimized. By the time the clouds started their journey back home sometime in the 2000s, the possibility of acid rain had reduced manifold.

***

When they reached their familiar forest, they felt a surge of energy and happiness again. They rushed ahead with gusto, ready to burst into rain, and waited for the welcoming sights and sounds they knew.

Would they be there?

A fluttering of wings startled the clouds as their old friend, the hornbill, appeared from nowhere, looking expectantly at them.

'Hornbill!' they cried. 'You came after all!'

'Of course I did!' said the hornbill. 'You're back here after so many years! We had other clouds here, but we missed you!'

'So did we, but we thought you'd have heard the news – that we'd caused the acid rain and all that—' began one cloud.

'Well, I know you better than anyone else,' said the hornbill, 'and I wouldn't believe any rumours anyway. And you should know that your name is all cleared now! The real culprits – the gas emissions from the factories – have been stopped in their tracks!'

The clouds were beside themselves with joy. The welcome chorus started – frogs croaking, elephants trumpeting – and what not! The clouds showed their happiness with a downpour.

Just before they floated away, they decided to ask the hornbill a niggling question: 'Uhh – Hornbill, is it true that you can drink water only when it rains?'

The hornbill laughed. 'Of course not,' it said. 'I don't need to drink any water at all. I get all the water I need from the fruits I eat.'

'Then why do you come each time we get ready to pour?' asked the confused clouds.

'Just for your sake,' said the hornbill, smiling. 'It always feels good to know that you have friends who wait for you!'

What was acid rain?

Acid rain was a man-made disaster that was averted just in time. Due to the heavy pollution caused by industries and factories, rain turned 'acidic' – meaning that rainwater was no longer a harmless, pure liquid. It had combined with other chemicals to become 'acid,' which tastes sour, and eats away skin and metal.

Some acids are strong and others are weak. A good example of acid is the gastric juice in our stomach, which breaks down the food we eat and kills bacteria. Fruits also contain acids like citric acid in citrus fruits (such as lemons and oranges), and maleic acid in apples. Vinegar, which we use to preserve food and to enhance flavour, is also an acid (acetic acid). However, these are weak acids, hence we are able to consume them in moderate quantities.

But acid rain contained strong acids (which should not be tasted or touched!). Like all acids, it had high amounts of hydrogen ions. When industrial gases (specifically sulphur dioxide and nitrogen oxide), caused by burning of fossil fuels like coal, combine with water and oxygen in the atmosphere, they transform into sulphuric acid and nitric acid (two strong acids!), which form acidic droplets in clouds and fall as rain or snow.

While the phenomenon was discovered in 1963 by American ecologist Gene Likens, it took various studies and experiments to confirm the cause and effects of acid rain. Acid rain destroyed forests in Europe, completely wiped out life in lakes in North America, and damaged human health and crops in Asia. Even the Taj Mahal in India turned yellow because of acid rain corroding the marble! Scientists worked hard to inform the heads of countries, and spread awareness all over the world to control pollution to prevent acid rain. As a result of various treaties and green initiatives adopted the world over, acid rain is no longer a threat.

ACKNOWLEDGEMENTS

From the time that I can remember, all that I've ever asked for are books. Reading got me under the skin and into the heads of a million fictional characters, and made my childhood magical, letting me dream a billion dreams and think a trillion thoughts.

Then it was no longer enough that I read stories. I wanted to write them too. Yet, it seemed like one of those things that as a child, you think you're perfectly capable of doing – and then you grow up and look down on the whole thing as a silly fantasy that sounds rather impossible. I'm surprised that despite all my misgivings and self-doubt, I held on to this far-fetched fantasy, and my books are finally seeing the light of day.

I think of all the kids who grew up to be 'successful' by adult standards but couldn't realize their childhood dreams; then I realize this is a miracle and a blessing, and that I have a lot to thank the Almighty for.

If God pulled me through to this end, there was my loving family pushing me towards it – my name as author on the book's cover is a result of a mother's penance. My mother, Shirley, made her whole life about me, so that I could achieve whatever I had set out to. My books are a testimony to her love and sacrifice, and she has always been that voice of strength and reassurance that got me through all my trials and challenges. My aunt, Asha, is the bibliophile who helped me follow in her footsteps, whose stories I looked forward to everyday from the time I was a child. Apart from my mother, she was the first one to read my stories and poetry, and inspire in me the confidence that I could, indeed, write.

My grandmother, Grace, who is a paradoxical treasure trove of affection, tradition, sarcastic wit and an attitude of glorious indifference to naysayers, is the reason I don't stop dreaming of more books to write and more challenges to take on. My uncle Santhosh and aunt Jolly are my silent pillars, whom I trust to speak up for me anytime I need them to.

I wonder what my grandfather, K.J. Joseph, who taught me to write, would be thinking now as he looks down upon me from heaven – I do hope I've done him proud.

It is difficult to find method in my madness, but two people whom I am proud to call all my own uncomplainingly stand by me and I'm glad to say they love me despite the various (sometimes unreasonable) goals I chase – my husband Vineeth (who has accepted most things about me wholeheartedly, and some, with resignation) and my son Vihann (who is too small to protest at the moment).

To all the above, I am ever grateful – for all they have done for me, and continue to do for me.

I thank my editor, Vatsala Kaul Banerjee, for believing in my stories, and working day and night to make *From Sea to Sky* and *From Root to Rain* perfect in every aspect. Dear Vatsala – it was your decision to read my submission that brought me this far, and I am ever grateful for everything you've done for me. I have learnt a lot from you, and I hope it reflects in all my future writing.

I thank my publishers, Hachette India, for seeing the potential in my stories and taking them to children all over the world. I thank Ishan Trivedi for the beautiful illustrations in the book that have brought my stories to life, and Sharanya Kunnath for the awesome cover design.

I also thank Usha Akella, well-known poet, who transformed my poetry through her crisp editing, giving me valuable lessons on how to improve my craft. Thank you, Usha!

I thank the *Hans India* newspaper, which carried my stories first as 'Nature Narratives' and gave me my first break as a regular columnist on the 'Young Hans' page. I thank Prof. K. Nageshwar, who was the then editor of the newspaper, for the opportunity, and Mr Ramu Sharma, the current editor, for granting me permission to compile my published stories as books.

I am grateful to the management and my colleagues at ICAR-CRIDA, Hyderabad, for all their support.

I remember all my friends from school to university, who read my stories, marvelled at them and assured me that one day I would be a proper author who would make them proud – thank you!

I thank all my teachers and professors, especially Ms Anita Naidu (Rosary Convent High School), Prof. K. Stevenson, Prof. K. Narender, Prof. Y.L. Srinivas and Prof. G.K. Subbarayudu (Osmania University) who always believed in me and encouraged me.

I thank all those – known and unknown – who have wished me well and played a role in bringing me to where I am today.

I thank all the children who will read my stories, and grow to love science and Nature through them. I hope that I can arouse in them the same magic that I felt as a child, and that they will be the reason that I write more stories, and more books.

After all, books are all that I've ever wanted. To read. And to write.

Liked *From Root to Rain*? Then you'll love this book too!

FROM SEA TO SKY

Hidden Stories of Nature's Science

by Sneha Verghese

***

Trees with 'ears'.
Mosquitoes that are saviours.
Octopuses that operate tools and hoard rubble.
A bird that pretends its way out of trouble.
Butterflies that leave ants in a daze.
A creature that can survive nuking, toxins and even outer space.
Birds obsessed with blue.
IS ALL THIS REALLY TRUE?

Find out all about these and more in this exciting collection of 25 fascinating stories that takes you up into the sky, under the oceans, over mountains, through forests and across the world in a way you never imagined.

Introducing eager young readers to amazing science in the environment around them, these tales break down complex concepts into easy-to-follow ideas, while answering questions, explaining scientific phenomena and sparking curiosity to explore the secret world of Nature.

Get set for a roller-coaster ride of thrilling discoveries!